T0064218

Rest in the Nest

Powerful Principles of Rest in Parenting

SONYA JUDD

WESTBOW
PRESS®
A DIVISION OF THOMAS NELSON
& ZONDERVAN

WestBow Press books may be ordered through booksellers or by contacting:

WestBow Press
A Division of Thomas Nelson & Zondervan
1663 Liberty Drive
Bloomington, IN 47403
www.westbowpress.com
844-714-3454

ISBN: 978-1-6642-2658-6 (sc)
ISBN: 978-1-6642-2657-9 (e)

Print information available on the last page.

WestBow Press rev. date: 03/18/2021

CONTENTS

Foreword... vii

Introduction: Stop Signs... ix

Chapter 1   Where It All Started 1

Chapter 2   Running on Fumes.. 6

Chapter 3   It's Just Too Hard... 9

Chapter 4   Understand Your Limitations...............................15

Chapter 5   From Negative Emotions to Positive Responses..... 18

Chapter 6   Biblical Rest.. 22

Chapter 7   Rest Versus Sleep 26

Chapter 8   Simple Fixes for Better Sleep 30

Chapter 9   Stimulants 32

Chapter 10 The TV Is Not My Friend.................................... 34

Chapter 11 The Enemy Encourages Exhaustion 38

Chapter 12 God Promises Us Rest 40

Chapter 13 Your Most Significant Relationships 44

Chapter 14 Holding the Calendar Accountable..................... 53

Chapter 15 Goals and Priorities.. 63

Chapter 16 Organization and Time Management.................... 65

Chapter 17 Counting the Costs: Family Finances 75

Chapter 18 Lost, Lonely Eyes: Making Decisions About Daycare 83

Chapter 19 Assembling [Your Name] 93

Appendix 95

FOREWORD

This book is my offering to God as a testimony of His sustenance and grace in my life. And for whom I am nothing without.

I dedicate this book to Samantha Renaa, Stephen Michael, and Serah Elyce Judd, who have proven to me that being a mom is the greatest and most fulfilling calling I know.

Lastly, I give honor and gratitude to my parents, who raised ten children to be, well, like us, in wisdom, love, and strong character. You could have warned me that this would be so hard. I'll have to get you for that.

INTRODUCTION: STOP SIGNS

It was like a dream, but I was awake. There was no milk. I had just enough money to get the other essentials until we got paid on Friday. My Irish-triplet toddlers (three under three) had just fallen asleep, so I only had thirty minutes to scoot to the store and back before they awoke from their 30-minute afternoon nap. I petitioned our neighbor's teen to watch them for a bit while I went to the store.

I started the car. I'm sure it started, but I don't remember hearing the engine. I cautiously backed out of the driveway. I savored the few scarce moments of peace and quiet, comforted by my little space to let my guard down.

As I drove slowly from our home to the edge of the subdivision, my thoughts drifted. When was the last time I was outside? We should cook more food on the grill. Is it time to cut the grass yet? My stomach growled, reminding me I had unintentionally skipped the last two meals. I didn't care. I sat at the stop sign, lost in my train of thought, looking at the sky and the cars passing by. How nice would it be to just sit here, doing nothing? The warmth of the car lulled me further into my thoughts.

A loud horn interrupted my oasis. In the car behind me, a man angrily waved his hands over the steering wheel, motioning me to go. I turned on my left signal and—now alert—proceeded into the intersection for my seven-minute ride to the local grocery store. As I recovered my wits, I realized I had fallen asleep at the stop sign.

I would not have believed it was possible to fall asleep at a stop sign. But sleep had seized the opportunity it was given, overtaking me in a mere sliver of rest. In that moment, I recognized the level of desperation into which I had allowed myself to sink. I couldn't remember sleeping longer than three hours in the last twelve months. The children were on a time schedule of their own design. When one child woke up, the others woke up too. It was a sadistic game they played with me. Although unintentional, it was nonetheless cruel. I had three-day old oatmeal stuck to my shirt (I hadn't showered in three days), my hair was sticking up on my head like a bird's nest, and my house had fallen victim to Hurricane Toddler. I felt emotionally bankrupt and defeated, borrowing moments at stop signs like money from loan sharks.

Trading the welfare of my children for my own meant I was too sleep-deprived to enjoy the precious moments of motherhood I was trying so hard to preserve. In retrospect, the problem was not that I had too many children, that I had children spaced too closely, or even that they were all so young. The issue was I had not prioritized rest as I should have. I forfeited hours of restoration, trying to "get ahead" instead of listening to my body. My gas tank had reached empty, and I didn't have the wherewithal to stop myself. Unfortunately, the repercussions of my perpetual sleepless stupor did not dawn on me until much later. More importantly, I did not realize the secret to recovery relied specifically on resting my soul and my body, by listening to my body's signals, and giving my body what it needed.

Rest in the Nest is the culmination of my experiences as a stay-at-home mom with babies and toddlers, learning lessons about rest a little later than I should have. I read plenty of parenting books, kept up with breastfeeding blogs, attended mommy support groups, and adored my children… but something was missing, and it took me by surprise.

My husband and I had chosen the path of parenthood—even designed it together. I would stay home while my husband worked outside of the home. Though we had planned it all out, being a mother wasn't exactly all I had imagined because of the lack of rest. The truth I want to share with you is sometimes raw and ugly, but I hope it will keep you from suffering the way I did.

This book is designed to encourage the weary, console the tired, and arm the hopeless with actionable strategies for getting and maintaining a restful existence in your home and your life.

Rest, which includes sleep, is a restorative process, just as activity constitutes an exhaustive process. Activity is necessary to express life, but it must be alternated with periods of rest; otherwise, we wear ourselves down, burning our candles from both ends. During the hours of rest and sleep, when we seem to be most passive, the restorative process within us is intensely active, recharging us with vital energy for the next day.

If we are to embrace rest, we have to understand the process of rest, know why rest is necessary, and how the process of sleep strengthens us. When we understand all this, we are more inclined to integrate rest intentionally into our lives. In doing so, we will reap benefits for ourselves and those around us.

1

Where It All Started

M y desire to be a mom evolved during college. Having grown up in a family of twelve, I longed for the strong bonds of friendship, unity, and togetherness in the loving environment of a tight-knit family. Leaving home for college in New York helped crystallize that desire. I longed for purpose—my purpose—and fulfillment.

As a result of the events of 9-11, I had a medical procedure that restored my body physically from trauma, but in doing so, jeopardized my fertility. A short time later, I met the man who would become my husband. Fully aware of the potential for childbearing challenges, he asked for my hand in marriage.

Two years into our marriage, we had not conceived, as my physician forewarned. Secretly, I longed for a child. The warmth of a large family defined my soul for so long that I felt naked without those close bonds. A few days before our three-year anniversary, our prayers were answered when I stared at a positive pregnancy test in my hand. We were filled with gratefulness and joy. Many days of silent prayers and grueling nights of tears in the closet, had been answered in a miraculous way.

At 20 weeks of my pregnancy, I was still fully engaged in my normal activities – working full-time, having minimal complications, exercising, and wearing the same clothes from pre-pregnancy. At a regular prenatal visit during my lunch break, the nurse was chatty as usual and began her examination. It wasn't unusual for her to proceed swiftly and quietly, so I did not notice immediately that her body language changed. She hopped from her chair and said, 'be right back.' A second nurse came in the room, and the two resumed the examination. I did not anticipate more than 15 minutes at the doctor's office and made a subtle joke about it taking so long. They didn't laugh. The second nurse left the room with a smile and said, 'be right back'. Where was everyone going?

The next few moments, that nurse returned with the obstetrician, and a box of tissues. It wasn't until then that I realized something was very wrong. The doctor had a kind smile but wasted little time on cordial pleasantries. His eyes stern and squinted, he went right to work observing the screen intensely. After a haptic vaginal examination, he took off his gloves and slowly exhaled 'you are about four centimeters dilated; you are losing the baby. In fact, I can see the foot. You need to call your husband so we can make a decision."

My husband arrived quickly, only to find two nurses and a doctor in the room, and his wife prostrate with fear as if a bomb had been dropped. The doctor repeated the admonition and added that we needed to make a decision based on one of three options. The first option was to have an emergency surgical cerclage (sewing the uterus closed similar to a purse pull string). This surgery posed a moderate risk since there was no clear indication of the cause of early dilation. He explained that if it turned out that the cause of pre-dilation was an infection, the cerclage would be of no affect, and could cause additional harm. The second option was to be admitted to the hospital at that moment for the duration of the pregnancy (24 weeks) in a slightly inverted position, utilizing gravity to hold the fetus inside. The third option of the highest risk was to go home and pray for a miracle. Obvious threats to ending the pregnancy due to pre-dilation included walking, sneezing, or coughing, either of which could trigger imminent miscarriage.

Without a huddle, we spoke simultaneously and without hesitation: "we will go home and pray".

We drove in silence to our 1-bedroom walkup apartment. I felt like crying, but didn't want to take the risk of complicating my condition. I lay flat on the bed as instructed and stayed that way for another week. My thoughts raced all day, every day. Why would a good God have given me a child, and then take it back? For what reason would God test my faith in this extreme manner, in the matter of a child's life? I went back and forth in my mind, wondering what I might have done wrong to receive such punishment. It was an exhausting exercise that rendered the same answer every single time: 'I don't know'.

One night as I was praying in my heart for the baby to live, I was reminded of the story of Abraham, Sarah and Isaac. You may recall Abraham was the leader of the Israelites in the Old Testament. God promised him and his wife Sarah, both beyond 90 years of age, a son from her own loins. That promised son did not come for a number of years, but God's promise did not fail. Sarah bore a son named Isaac when she was almost 100 years old. Abraham loved Isaac tremendously. One day, God told Abraham to go up on the mount and offer Isaac as a sacrifice. In obedience, Abraham tied Isaac up to sacrifice him. As he was lifting his knife to kill him, an angel stopped him, and the Lord provided a goat caught in the thicket as a sacrifice, instead of Isaac's life. (Genesis 22.1-19, NKJV)

As I read through this passage in the Bible, I began to understand the wisdom of God in granting a miracle, but ensuring we continued to serve Him as the Giver, and not replacing Him with the gift.

Through lots of love and support from friends and family, I remained pregnant at home until 22 weeks of gestation. A suite of specialists concurred by conference call with us to determine next steps for the pregnancy. We all agreed to admittance into the hospital to see if we could make it to at least 24 weeks, a minimum gestation required for a 17% chance of survival. On Easter morning at 12.21 a.m., my firstborn baby girl was delivered at twenty-three weeks, one pound seven ounces, and ten inches long (the length of a pencil). She had see-through skin and her eyes were fused shut. Her early exit from the womb had not allowed time for normal development, most importantly, of her major organs.

Modern medicine has not been able to reproduce the extraordinary mother's womb. Our firstborn lived in an incubator for the next 137 days. I would visit the hospital once or twice a day to hold this tiny human inside of my clothes, as my scent and my heartbeat simulated the womb, causing her to relax and heal better and quicker. It was painstaking to come home without her at night, having held her so close for hours.

Over the next four months, there were nightly visits to the hospital for more kangaroo care and breast milk delivery. Frequent doctor reports indicating details of her delicate and acute condition left us oscillating between hope and despair.

Finally, she was released to come home at three months of age. Spacing pregnancies was not in God's game plan for our family, as less than a month after that, we discovered that we had conceived again… and this time, we were expecting twins.

Since our first child was developmentally four months behind, and the twins came a month early, we virtually had triplets, also known as "Irish triplets." God answered my prayers in a miraculous way. In the span of a year, we went from a childless married couple, to now parents of three children.

Our quiver was full! The joys of parenthood were realized. Now to figure out how this parenting thing worked. Not fully understanding what we were doing and how we should operate, we dove headfirst into raising our children. We'd read lots of articles, talked to plenty of seasoned parents, and had a good upbringing ourselves. We've got this! Yeah, sure, we had it alright. Soon, we were overrun with babies, bills, and bottles. I quit my job to take care of the children full-time, so we were reduced from a dual- to single-income household. We had also purchased a home for our expanding family, which was an extra financial stressor. On top of everything, as parents we were now outnumbered two-to-three. With no family nearby to help, we had to figure out how to make things work ourselves. This included:

➤ considering the benefits and consequences of childcare versus staying at home
➤ distributing responsibilities to divide and conquer areas of parenthood
➤ avoiding becoming so preoccupied with managing three children that we forgot to enjoy our blessed new life!

Most parents can relate to hardships during the early childhood years. Very few people are prepared for the challenges in faith, uncooperative finances, and the pressure on marriage that parenthood brings. On the other hand, navigating through the obstacles that present themselves during this phase can also be a time of personal maturity and immense growth for you, and those watching you.

We didn't know at the time, but a lack of rest and sleep were at the root of a lot of the frustration and conflict we experienced during these years. Rest, a word related but not synonymous with sleep, implies a deeper serenity in spite of our circumstances and a stability of mind, soul, and body. With rest there is peace, and with peace there is stability and joy in the home.

Key Takeaways

- Sometimes God tests our faith in Him through challenges with the very gifts He grants. Our children are precious gifts from God. Relying on Him above all else is foundational to our child's wellbeing.
- No one is completely prepared for parenting. Start where you are, dig deep, and trust your instincts. Maturity and growth are natural outcomes where you are consistently learning.
- A lack of sleep and rest could be at the root of conflict and frustrations. When tensions are exacerbated and irritability arises, check your rest barometer to ensure you are giving yourself the best chance at managing everything.

2

Running on Fumes

"I am only one, but I am one. I cannot do everything, but
I can do something; and what I should do and can do, by
the grace of God, I will do." — Author Unknown

Perfectionism prevented me from reaching success early on as a wife and
mom. I wanted my life to be a vignette straight out of a magazine. I
was obsessed with fulfilling each child's every need as soon as it presented
itself, making sure they looked their best for others all the time, and
corralling them into acting as well-behaved as possible.

One of my biggest mistakes was placing my children's welfare above
my own. Putting your children first sounds heroic in writing, but in
practice, it can actually become prideful. Your work at making sure your
children are experiencing their best life can subtly slip into an area of pride
and arrogance, that your children are better than others. If you are not
careful to maintain the proper order of God, spouse, yourself, and then
the children, you may notice an imbalance in other areas of your life. And
when we are not trusting in God for parenting, we can subtly implicitly or
explicitly exalt ourselves for the achievements and structure of our family,
our parenting, or our children.

My day would start when the sun rose with feedings. My husband was
working an "eight-to-five" job. The children would awake about every four
hours for feedings. We agreed to rotate sleeping and feedings on the kids'
schedule, which allowed my husband some sleep before going to work. But
the children made no such promise. Very quickly, I learned that four-hour

segments of time for sleep and rest does not suffice in the middle of all the other chores that seem small on their own but add up.

My attempted schedule included feeding babies, changing diapers, sleep-training, intentional playtime, baths, and soothing the woes of toddlers. In between that schedule, I searched high and low for opportunities to shower myself, eat real food, or—on a heavenly occasion—nap. I think by now, you can predict that the plan didn't work.

Slowly but surely, my expressed personal needs diminished to primitive instincts. Showering was a privilege every three to four days. Hot meals were no longer required; in fact, sitting down during meals was rare. Creating a healthy, safe, and Godly home for my children took priority over everything. Leftover moments were stolen by repairs to the house, dirty dishes, overstuffed diaper genies, and beaver dams of laundry.

Fatigue from the mental activity was worse than the toll of the physical exhaustion. I was constantly second-guessing myself. I was conscious of not only my indecision, but also the time and energy it cost me to be confused. Laundry stacked up because I literally sat, weighing the pros and cons of running to the store for detergent or taking a powernap. Dishes went undone because I did not know how to break down the task into small sections. Car maintenance and housing chores were so poorly prioritized that only during a crisis did I recognize their importance.

After a while, my hair started to fall out. I avoided social interaction because I didn't feel presentable. My only nutrition came from coffee and bananas. (Coffee is a helper sometimes but can often be the barrier between you and rest if not consumed in moderation.)

It's one thing to know you need rest, and another to actually implement restful practices. Resources like family, friends, or babysitters are a privilege, not a guarantee. With few close friends, family far away, and no money for a sitter, I did not have a strong network from which to draw resources. My husband was doing what he thought would help. When he got home from work, he would play with the children, creating a jungle gym in the middle of the living room. Cackles of laughter and glee filled every room of the house. Every now and then he'd cook some of his finest entrees - Fettuccine Alfredo with shrimp and eggplant, or steaks on the grill. I could even coax him into painting a room or helping me put away the toys. Although he tried, his efforts did not seem like enough. I was frustrated, tired, and—to be transparent—angry. I blamed him for not helping me more, mainly because he was the only other adult around to catch the heat. As unfair and irrational as it may seem, separation and resentment chipped away at my already fragile emotions.

Experts always recommend a safety net for yourself before you start trying to save others—like putting on your own oxygen mask in a plane emergency before helping someone else. Another example: when you are paid, the first thing you should do is pay yourself by rewarding yourself with self-care, investing in retirement, or putting some away in savings. Only after that should one pay bills or give money to others. But when we are exhausted and discouraged, we tend to rationalize making other tasks and people our priority.

Remember: it is not expected of you to continue a grueling schedule day in and day out without rest. You need to take your own health seriously. It is easy to become a victim of your circumstances if you continue placing others' welfare above your own.

Key Takeaways

- Don't allow perfectionism to delay progress.
- Avoid placing your child's welfare above your own.
- Put away any pride that prevents you from getting the help you need (and deserve).

3

It's Just Too Hard

"It is good to have a destination to walk towards; but it is the journey that matters in the end." –Le Guin

Personal Journal Entry

Today was a particularly hard day. After weeks and weeks of day-in and day-out care for the babies, I fear my mind has turned to mush. I have a nervous tiredness that keeps my stomach in knots so that my appetite is held at bay. I'm always just on the verge of crying, daily contemplating the worth of my existence. I cannot seem to get my pickiest eater to eat vegetables, and the twins are surviving on whatever fuel I can muster up from a three- to four-hour sleep period last night.

Around 2 o'clock I had no idea what to prepare for lunch. I wish we had more money for food. Why won't God answer me? Like a chorus, they all started crying. I feel so much grief and anger towards them, towards myself, and towards God. I wanted to grab one of them and shake them for crying so loud. My mind raced ferociously. I took each child up to their room and put them in their crib and shut the door. They screamed bloody murder.

I felt that strange sinking feeling in the pit of my stomach. You know, the kind that makes you look both ways as if a train is coming. The thought of what I was about to do sent chills down my spine as a draft seep[ed] into my untidy blouse. I grabbed my wallet and my car keys and jumped into the van and cranked it. The dichotomy of my love for my children and the desperate need to get away was tormenting. Resigned and defeated to the responsibility of motherhood, I sank my face into my hands and wept bitterly. Unable to hold back any emotion, I poured out my heart. Everything inside of me wanted to drive away and never return.

As the van idled, I looked at the lonely white door that leads into the house. Hugging the steering wheel, my body trembled in utter failure and fatigue under the continuing stream of tears. It felt like hours—no, days—passed before I was able to come up for air.

I do not have the option of giving up. They have only me. I wish they were given another choice in the matter. I was given to them, not someone else, so I must have something to offer that no one else can.

After three or four deep, drawn breathes, I stopped crying. I looked at the door. Somehow, I made the decision to keep going one more day. I turned the van off to go inside. It was only then that I noticed I had no shoes on, no coat, nor was I wearing my glasses.

These were my early days of being a stay-at-home mom. Parenting is a fulfilling gift, one of the greatest callings one can have. But it's not always easy. Although your thoughts and emotions might make you feel like you are going to die, you are not. You are not at the end of your rope, or alone, or going crazy. A crisis, by definition, is temporary. Persevere a little more to find that patch of relief. Raising children will not be difficult forever.

Kids grow up. Each day of parenting contributes to their maturation and development. What you are pouring into them will be reflected in some doses now and more holistically in later years, and you will see the benefit of your hard work.

The role of the parent (especially the stay-at-home parent) is minimized by the media and within the corporate world because it is compared to success in business, profits, and personal ambition. This unfair comparison undermines the important role of parents as teachers, nurturers, trainers, and protectors. Sometimes these mischaracterizations create discontent to the point of discouragement. Practice affirmations to protect your heart from falling into the enemy's lies:

o I am the heartbeat of the family.
o I am exactly where God wants me to be.
o I am here on purpose, and my position is of the highest value.
o I can do this! My children need me and deserve my best.
o I love these children. And they love me.
o I will keep going. To give up is not an option.

Whenever possible, seek help if you need it. Borrow, budget, or trade for time or money from friends, colleagues, neighbors, or family to see a counselor or therapist, or to book a babysitter. Reserve a couple hours for yourself—a walk outside, a date night, prayer, or for handwriting a note or card for someone.

Allow yourself grace to be vulnerable enough to say when it gets too hard. It is safe and brave to acknowledge when it gets too hard. Most often people really want to help but 'need permission' or are unaware that you need it until you indicate as much. Being vulnerable in this way alerts others to jump into action to provide what you need when you need it. Nothing takes the place of rest. It is not a luxury, but a requirement. As a parent, you don't have weekends or holidays or sick days off. You don't get a raise or a promotion; you don't even get paid, unless you count being paid in handmade drawings, noodle necklaces, hugs and kisses. You will not get monetarily rich in this role. But the benefits are priceless and far outweigh the costs.

As diet and exercise are to weight loss, so is parenting the young to seeing them grown up. The results are not always visible or immediate, but when they manifest, you will be amazed. Imagine your child becoming well-mannered because you took the time to teach them to say 'thank you' or 'it's nice to meet you'. Or when they fix their beds all by themselves and are so proud because they have seen you do it so well. What about when they are young adults who volunteer their time and efforts for those in need without your prompting? Savor the day you will overhear them speaking life and encouragement to their friend who has gone down a wrong path and reaped hard consequences. Whether you see them in their career as a doctor or writer, a teacher, or singer, you will remember the times you encouraged them to cultivate the gifts and talents they are uniquely equipped with. Your many hours of doing homework and reading with them, laughing at yourself with them, or sacrificing money for housewares to buy that favorite toy, and every school performance contributes to who they are and will be in the future. Even imagine your preschooler praying for daddy to get a new job because they believe by faith that God is omnipotent and good.

Your child may not realize the depths you have gone to help mold their character, but they will very likely see glimpses of your brilliance, grace, kindness, forgiveness, dedication, and selflessness that will impact them in ways you may never know. Look for evidence of your influence in perhaps their choices in friends, reading material, or music. Watch closely as they struggle through putting together toys that break, or pass that swim test after the third try, or cry their way through their lovesick broken heart – and you'll see the grit and resilience you thought they never noticed in you. How will you feel on their wedding day when they marry a person whose character is above reproach, and who enters a marriage of love and honor 'just like my parents'?

You are raising little people who will emulate what they see in their environment. You are the object of their affection. They want to please you desperately. Their plan is to make you laugh hysterically. Smiling at them shares an admirable glow of 'I love you and accept every single part of you.' If you look closely, you can see it in their eyes. Your appeasing gaze disarms them in ways other things or people cannot.

Don't think you've made a positive impression? That somehow your child got cheated out of better parents and got you instead? That you've made mistakes that will scar them for life? Truthfully, there is no exact formula for great parenting. We have all made mistakes, big ones and little ones, and a lot of in-between ones. What is right for one parent, may not be effective for another parent. Thankfully, life has an amazing way balancing the weights. Where we lack, a friend, future colleague of theirs, future mate, neighbor, mentor, or a teacher could provide connecting links to solutions.

These are only a few of the many benefits of parenting. The joy, the fulfillment, and the delight come when you least expect it. They occur as a result of your planning, toil, tears, confusion, frustration, sacrifice, doubts, and fears. We will discuss feelings of inadequacy later in the book, but those emotions are very real and could be deterrents to progress.

You will optimize best results if and when you take (not make) time to rest and get help to do so. As you make it a point to find the help you need, you will have the time and brain power to think through how to improve the care of the children, the home, and yourself. Like any job, there are stages of learning by which we acclimate to the new role. In your team of one, or two, or eighteen (parent(s), children, in-laws, grandparents, etc.), iterative adjustments need to be made to adapt to the ever-changing dynamic within the house—schedules, personalities, energy levels, and typical breaking points need to be considered. The objective is to find ways to manage the lives in your household with effectiveness and efficiency so you can rest and sleep.

Key takeaways

- Acknowledge your need for help, quickly. Find, create, or beg for a network of supporters who can provide short and extended time spans of time for your reprieve.
- Blessings of parenthood far outweigh any costs of being a parent.
- Current business environments and social media outlets devalue the role of parents. Internalize affirmations to encourage yourself and dispel such falsehoods.
- Take (not make) time for yourself – a walk, journaling, or engaging in your favorite hobby.

- It is safe and courageous to acknowledge when it gets too hard. Most people want to help but "need permission" or are unaware that you need it. Being vulnerable in this way alerts others to jump into action to provide what you need when you need.
- You may not immediately see the fruits of your labor during early childhood parenting, but they will ripen in due season.

4

Understand Your Limitations

We spend a third of our lives in sleep, and its recuperative effects are amazing. But it is not always necessary to sleep in order to obtain these beneficial results. Rest will revitalize us as well...if it is the right kind of rest.

What do I mean by "rest"? Rest is simply choosing to refrain from activities that exhaust you. More specifically, restful activities that are not sleep include sitting quietly and just thinking. For some, it could be meditating or praying. For others, resting could include reading a book, bird watching, driving a long distance, or doing puzzles. Activities that tend to exhaust most people could be changing cat litter for a third time during the day. Or wrestling rush hour traffic. Doing household chores for most parents tops the list of exhaustive activities, but so might talking to friends or family members on the phone. The difference in the restful and exhaustive activities is your mind's perception of that activity being chaotic or calming, a drain or a driver, emotionally taxing or peaceful. Your brain accepts that emotion from your psyche, tells your body "you won't like this; this is bad!" or "this will soothe you. This is good!' And your body responds to that message with tension that exhausts you or pacifiers that calm you.

Normal rest and sleep produce alertness. The daily duties of parenting need to be calibrated by your body's signals. Just as your body signals that it is time to rest, it will also signal when you have reached your limit in day-to-day work. However, do you listen to your body's signals? It's easy to fall into the trap of running so fast we deny ourselves sound judgment. You have the greatest advantage since you know your body better than anyone else in the world. Your body's main communication will usually come from your soul – your own conscience – saying 'lay down, you're tired. Rest.' Or 'that's enough'. If we're driven to succeed, tormented by the possibility of failing (or being perceived by others as failing), or beguiled by perfectionism, we tend to ignore these warnings. Those that are close to us are often used to bring our condition to our attention if they believe we are risking more than we should.

Heed signs that you've overextended yourself:

- Eyes: dark circles appear; redness or strain on the eyes. Obvious signs of fatigue like droopy eyes or falling asleep in unintentional places or times.
- Your reactions to miniscule things catalyze stronger emotion than warranted.
- Your reflexes are slower, maybe one or two beats off your natural pace.
- Your desire to rest outweighs the desire to eat.
- Atypical clumsiness: you trip over things, drop things, or mishandle objects, more easily managed during well-rested times.
- Some or all of the above.

When we are well-rested, we are cognizant of our surroundings and obligations, and take the steps necessary to find effective solutions for problems without going overboard.

Don't feel pressured to commit when you are unable to, financially or emotionally or physically. Over-committing is a serious mistake because it is rooted in trying to please others despite limitations. When people go beyond their limitations, they develop a sense of shame for not achieving the impossible. Reject notions of guilt for not being able to accomplish all that you want to; instead, give yourself grace.

Indications you're overcommitted include:

o   a constant temptation or habit of cancelling plans.
o   leaving engagements early.
o   the inability to focus or be fully present in what you're doing.

o running out of time for important self-care rituals like showering, reading, journaling, and/or exercising.

Try to be realistic about how much time you have to commit to these tasks and goals. When self-evaluation reveals you're overextended, stop and regroup. Reject feelings of guilt; they are misplaced and don't add any value.

Key takeaways

- It is not always necessary to sleep in order to obtain the beneficial results of revitalization. Rest will as well if it is the right kind of rest.
- Rest is choosing to refrain from activities that exhaust you. They depend on your personal motivators and detractors but could include things like meditating or reading. Exhaustive activities are also personal but might include washing dishes or speaking on the phone to a long-winded friend.
- Listen to your body signals to rest when you have reached your limit.
- Over-committing is rooted in trying to please others despite limitations.

5

From Negative Emotions to Positive Responses

Overworking or prolonged physical strain wastes energy. But emotions are even more important than our body's actions and work. All strong emotions have the same effect. Fear, worry, anxiety, anger, and similar powerful emotions consume an inordinate amount of usable energy, reducing reserves for use in the body.

Just as powerful feelings can drain energy from cells rapidly, less powerful ones—sustained over a period of time—will exhaust them slowly. Worrying prompts your body to produce the adrenaline-like chemical epinephrine, which keeps you awake. Fears and unforgiveness in particular have this effect, as do frustrations, resentments, and inner disharmonies. These will fight against one another and ultimately devitalize our bodies completely.

To properly process the emotions that can steal your energy, try, whenever possible, to choose to see the good in everything you do. Change your posture to gratitude for your life and blessings to become more positive and energized. Instead of being upset that the milk was spilled on the carpet, respond to your child and within your heart: "Oopsie daisy! Well thank God we've got milk to spill. Thank you, Lord, for nutrition for my children." Or when your children are sick, pray for their health and end the prayer in thanksgiving and reminiscence: "Lord, thank You for healing my child. You've made her so beautiful and kindhearted and sweet-tempered. I love her eyes and soft skin. She makes me laugh when…"

Your emotions are all guided by your individual perspective. Changing your perspective may be the remedy for those baby blues and spurts of discontent.

God has already equipped you to do everything He has called you to do at this moment. He has given you the privilege of raising children for His purpose because He knew you were worthy of the calling. Your mistakes are His opportunities to train you, just as you train your children. There is no one more qualified to do what you are doing in the world. You are important. You are relevant. You are chosen.

Walking in the Spirit is one of the most important ways to manage emotional stimulus for the busy parent. Walking in the Spirit addresses your heart attitude toward God, others, and your life. The opposite of walking in the Spirit is walking in the flesh, which is more reactive and less thoughtful. In the flesh, our emotions tend to supersede reason, and we are generally self-serving. Often fleshly decisions rely on lower vibrational energies of jealous, rage, envy, pride, unforgiveness, hatred and the like.

When fear threatens to rob us of our sleep, peace of mind, or relationship with God, remember that fear comes from the enemy. David is such a great example of the dichotomy of courage as a warrior, and fearful as a leader in great consternation. In Psalm 55:1-8 (KJV), David expresses his fear and sorrow for the conspiracy of his son, Absalom, and the mutiny of his own people. Even though he was a man of boldness and courage, his heart was seized by fear at the imminent danger to his life. Fearfulness of mind can come upon us when we feel inadequate; when we feel we are failing as parents; when we are unable to re-enter the workforce because we've been out of it for so long; and when our bodies don't respond as we wish to exercise and multiple diets. We shift back and forth between fear and faith. Sometimes we have faith like David proudly proclaiming, "What can man do to me?" But at other times, our fears prevail and hover over us, as we take cover behind a façade.

King David was so distracted by fear, he wished he could fly away, saying, "O that I had wings like a dove!" (Psalm 55:6, WBT). Observe here how David desired his escape—on "wings like a dove." He did not wish for magnificent wings that would take him away swiftly, like a hawk, eagle, or other bird of prey. A dove flies low and takes shelter as soon as she can. This is the escape David wished from the Lord. His aim was not victory, but rest. "I would fly away and be at rest" (v.6). Peace, quietness, and solitude are what the wisest of men have coveted. When they are vexed and wearied with deep emotion, fearful of circumstances, and uncertainty about the future, they retire to a place of rest.

Earlier I shared a vulnerable moment from my early childhood parenting days from my personal journal. In those moments, fear gripped me like a horror film, and denied me the consoling assurance that it was all just make-believe (FEAR acronym = False Evidence Appearing Real). Bereft of logical options, flight seems safe and easy, even right. But intense fear is a paralytic fungus feeding on insecurities like maggots. It typically strikes after festering beneath our mistakes and discouragement to capitalize on our compromised strength.

To desire escape from fears as David did is normal and expected. But running away does not solve the problem and could very well exacerbate them. Furthermore, escape is not sustainable; wherever you go, you are also there. Issues persist until we deal with them. What you do with the malignancy of fear, despondency, and helplessness, is what matters most to your recovery from them. I've found it most effective to find a way to release the torment through a positive active outlet that yields the relief sought. Crying, screaming into a pillow, yelling in the garage allows you to express how you feel without judgment or restraint. Other physical activities like running, biking, or aerobics release the tension from your body, bringing you back to a more relaxed state. I would recommend journaling or calling a trustworthy confidante. I wish I had known of these remedies earlier. I am already hyper, and an excitable state frightens even my bravest of friends. But they may work well for you and are worth trying.

Key takeaways:

- Strong emotions like fear, unforgiveness, and anger consume usable energy and reduce reserves the body uses.
- To properly process the emotions that can steal your energy, choose to see the good in everything you do. Adjust your posture to gratefulness.

- God has already equipped you to do everything He has called you to do at this moment.
- Walking in the Spirit is one of the most important ways to function for the busy parent.
- F.E.A.R. = False Evidence Appearing Real
- To desire escape from fears as David did is normal and expected. But running away does not solve problems and could very well exacerbate them.

6

Biblical Rest

The Bible is packed with examples of God's provisional rest. Even in creating the world, God rested on the seventh day not because He needed to, but because rest is important to Him. Let's dive into some verses that talk about rest.

When the Scripture refers to rest, it is often referring to rest in the context of relief in battle from enemies. Many biblical figures were literally running from deadly enemies, and others from false teachers, tyrannical governments, or false gods. Let's apply the same references to the fear and exhaustion the enemies of our soul's peace and rest.

In the book of Joshua, we learn Moses was succeeded by Joshua in leading the people of Israel in conquering their enemies. The land of Canaan was promised by God, but it was their responsibility to defeat the enemies within the land in order to settle it. Throughout the book of Joshua, God promised to deliver their enemies into their hands, as He did repeatedly. Finally, having destroyed the opposition thoroughly, God gave Joshua "rest all about" (Joshua 21:44 NKJV).

A similar reference is applied to David when he defeated the Philistines who were enemies to his settlement in the throne in 2 Samuel. The Lord gave King David "rest round about" from all those that were enemies to his settlement in the throne, and he set himself to enjoy that rest. (2 Samuel 7.1 NKJV). Although David was a man of war, he was in his element when he was at rest.

If we were having a conversation in your home and I said to you, 'hey friend, how are you doing? How are you really doing", what would be your response? What enemies lurk just beneath the surface in your life? What troubles you in your thoughts at night?

The after-battle state for both David and Joshua refers to a quiet and undisturbed rest. The landscape of our lives may not be physical battles on the field, but could include the war between resilience and surrender, ailments in our body, loneliness, or any number of competing deterrents of parenthood. We learn through David and Joshua's example we can savor in this same undisturbed rest God grants.

A divergent example is Solomon, David's son. Because David was a man of war, Solomon was delegated with the honorable task of building God's temple that his father designed. Solomon was a man of peace and that peace afforded him the opportunity to rest. (1 Kings 5:4, 1 Chronicles 22.9 NKJV) God's purpose was that the man that builds the temple should be a man of rest, and therefore should not have his time or thoughts diverted from his business. He should have rest from his enemies abroad, and he should have peace and quietness at home—allowing him the time and space to build the temple. Peace is a natural product of rest and goes hand in hand with a stillness that allows us to hear best from God. We can rely on the fact that He uses these moments to share His heart with us, to comfort us, and provide clarity on issues of the heart.

You may have been appointed by God to do the work of a parent for a specific reason. But you were chosen for the specific reason that God felt you could get it done. Put another way, you were nominated and won! So, He paves the way for rest, so you can work at parenting. Curious enough, it seems like where God provides rest, He expects work.

Let's read another passage, 2 Samuel 7:

"Now then, tell my servant David, 'This is what the LORD Almighty says: I took you from the pasture, from tending the flock, and appointed you ruler over my people Israel. I have been with you wherever you have gone, and I have cut off all your enemies from before you. Now I will make your name great, like the names of the greatest men on earth. And I will provide a place for my people Israel and will plant them so that they can have a home of their own and no longer be disturbed. Wicked people will not oppress them anymore, as they did at the beginning and have done ever since the time I appointed leaders over my people Israel. I will also give you rest from all your enemies'" (2 Samuel 7:8-11, NIV).

After defeating his enemies, David finds the permanent location for the Ark of the Covenant. In return, God is pleased and provides rest for him and his troops.

I want you to read that passage again, but imagine the Lord is speaking to you instead of David. Here is how I might apply it to my life:

"I took you from the pasture, from tending the flock, and appointed you ruler over my people Israel..." (2 Samuel 7:8 NIV).

The Lord specifically appointed me to take care of my children. His people are my responsibility and care.

"I have been with you wherever you have gone, and I have cut off all your enemies from before you" (2 Samuel 7:9a NIV).

He has been with me from the beginning, protecting me from enemies unseen—though I may struggle, perhaps He is protecting me in other ways—we have enough food on our table, beds to rest in, cars to drive, health and love.

"Now I will make your name great, like the names of the greatest men on earth" (2 Samuel 7:9b NIV).

My name, mother or father, is such an important, special name. The Lord has blessed me with parenthood because He wants me to prosper and glorify Him.

"And I will provide a place for my people Israel and will plant them so that they can have a home of their own and no longer be disturbed. Wicked people will not oppress them anymore, as they did at the beginning and have done ever since the time I appointed leaders over my people Israel" (2 Samuel 7:10-11a NIV).

The Lord is looking ahead of my family's path and preparing a safe, wonderful home for our children. When we love and nurture our children to be godly Christ-followers, they are better protected from the enemy's traps.

"I will also give you rest from all your enemies" (2 Samuel 7:11b NIV).

When I follow the path of the Lord, He will grant me rest for all that I will do for the kingdom.

A relatively calm and peaceful life will ensure longevity; and in the meantime, will ensure freedom from nervous depletion and breakdown. Remember: your life has a purpose. You are fulfilling at least one of God's purposes right now. You have been chosen to direct, educate, encourage, train, and nurture a human being—a person who is helpless now without you. A being that in a matter of eighteen years will be sent out into this world with a toolbelt full of everything you have imparted to him or her (the good and the bad) and will be asked to fend for himself or herself with those tools.

Key takeaways:

- Rest is important to God, as shown throughout the Bible.
- With David and Joshua's example we can savor in this same undisturbed rest God grants.
- You were chosen for the specific reason that God felt you could get it done.
- The Lord has blessed you with parenthood because He wants you to prosper and glorify Him.
- You have been chosen to direct, educate, encourage, train, and nurture a human being – it is a privilege!

7

Rest Versus Sleep

Internal and physical rest are fundamental requisites for a healthy life. Rest can be divided into four categories:

o   physical rest (discontinuing physical activity, going to bed, or relaxing)
o   sensory rest (being quiet and closing the eyes, no stimulation)
o   mental rest (quieting the mind from high emotional rigor)
o   physiological rest (an internal mellowness of the organs and internal functions of the physical body from activity such as digestion or fasting).

Rest is the inaction that prepares you for future action. People should not be ashamed of lying down, closing their eyes, and relaxing for a few minutes during the day. A small respite rests the heart, equalizes blood flow, and restores energy to the brain and nerve cells. It will prevent you from becoming fatigued.

Research shows varying nuances of the state of rest. Though some associate rest with sleeping, and others with meditative silence, it is really based on the state in which you scale significantly back from your typical forward momentum of activity to a point where you feel relaxed and emotionally free of negative thoughts. What one may consider restful—watching television, reading a book, or sitting in a chair with a cup of tea to think—another may consider not restful. Rest is measured by your normal day-to-day activity (which can be highly stressful), and the tranquility and slowed pace required to refresh yourself.

Sleep is a state in your brain and occurs in stages. As Katy News suggests in an article concerning getting better sleep: "It starts as you are first falling asleep, and your mind is turning off conscious awareness. Your body then starts going through different sleep cycles." With different ages come different needs, meaning some require more time to finish sleep cycles. While you are resting, your body is hard at work—storing memories, repairing muscles, and regulating hormones for growth, sleep, appetite, and more. "These things cannot happen during a short nap or rest. Deep restorative sleep is essential."[1]

The energy we exert should be rationed like precious treasure. Careful attention to our energy levels can prevent overtiredness and help us calibrate the activity in our life that best fits our physical condition. If we are overly active in our duties and leisure activity, the energy must be replenished accordingly. If not, we run into trouble. Overactivity could come in the form of working too many hours in the home or at our jobs, which includes working two or more jobs. Another example might be getting up before 6a, working all day, kid or parent activities in evenings, jumping back online at night, and checking social media in late hours. None of these activities are bad, and all of them contribute positively to us and our family when taken in moderation. But constant overexertion without taking an inventory of the hours we spend not resting can take a toll on our physical bodies.

Overwork and prolonged strain waste our energies. Emotions, especially strong emotions like anger, frustration, and fear, short-circuit the nervous system and exhaust our reserves quickly.

Have you ever exercised and felt totally refreshed afterward? But then you washed dishes and felt completely spent? The difference between these two activities is that in the former scenario, the body is working in tandem—as a unit. Whereas in the latter activity, mind and emotion are not in agreement with the physical body. In essence, the conscious mind is forcing the body to perform the activity while the subconscious mind

---

[1] "What's the Difference Between Sleep and Rest?" *The Katy News*, 18 Aug. 2020, thekatynews.com/2020/08/18/whats-the-difference-between-sleep-and-rest/.

and physical body are working against it. This internal conflict wears down the energy of the nerve cells.

As another example, a person who enjoys gardening can spend all day replanting and feel relatively fresh at the end of it; whereas if he vacuums for ten minutes, he is exhausted. In the first instance, the whole body is working in unison, whereas in the latter case, he is fighting against himself because his conscious mind forces him to perform the activity while his subconscious mind is resenting and resisting it. The result is that he is like two mules hitched to opposite ends of a rope, pulling against each other. They go nowhere. But hitch them in tandem, and they will carry loads for miles. It is this internal emotional conflict that wears down the energy of the nerve cells and in time produces dire results.

Adequate sleep, between six and eight hours, is necessary, especially if you need to rise early. It is best to measure your energy clock and determine what your storage capacity is. If your energy storage capacity is fifteen hours (6:00 a.m. to 9:00 p.m.), then the sixteenth hour will fatigue you far more than the first fifteen of the waking day, with more and more severe exhaustion with each additional hour. These hours past your energy reserves make all the difference between a normal life and one headed for ultimate physical and mental trouble.

According to studies conducted by the National Sleep Foundation,[2] only 25 percent of Americans get at least eight hours of sleep on weekdays, and 60 percent of women say they often sleep poorly. Researchers have determined that skimping on sleep has a price, including weight gain, diminished immune responses, lack of concentration, irritability, and depression.

Our culture undervalues sleep, which is why comparatively few people receive it. Stress and activity make us feel like we "can't turn our brain off," which is closer to the truth than we think.

---

[2] Hirshkowitz, PhD, Max. "National Sleep Foundation's Sleep Time Duration Recommendations: Methodology and Results Summary." *Sleep Health*, Journal of National Sleep Foundation, 15 Mar. 2015, www.thensf.org/sleep-health-journal/.

Key takeaways:

- Rest can be divided into four categories, physical, sensory, mental, physiological.
- Rest is the inaction that prepares you for future action versus sleep that occurs in stages in your brain
- While you are resting, your body is hard at work.
- Careful attention to our energy levels can prevent overtiredness and help us calibrate the activity in our life that best fits our physical condition.
- Emotions, especially anger, frustration, and fear, short-circuit the nervous system and exhaust our reserves quickly.
- It is this internal emotional conflict that wears down the energy of the nerve cells and in time produces agonizing results.
- Sleeping between six and eight hours is necessary.
- Hours beyond your energy reserves make the difference between a normal life and one headed for ultimate physical and mental trouble.
- Researchers have determined that skimping on sleep could cause weight gain, diminished immune responses, lack of concentration, irritability, and depression.

8

Simple Fixes for Better Sleep

So far, we've learned to embrace the joys of early childhood parenting by incorporating the rest and sleep our bodies so desperately require. We've also seen the all-too-personal results of misappropriating our energy towards the needs of others, when our body begs for rest. But there may be other impediments to the blessing of rest and sleep that may be hidden in plain sight. Harvard Medical School Women's Health Watch suggests areas that may also affect your sleep.

- **Physical conditions** such as high blood pressure or diabetes. Agitation or insomnia may camouflage concerning symptoms, but if caught early, they are treatable. Doctor checkups that include a full battery of tests can unmask clues to possible health concerns we may have ignored. Schedule these visit in advance and treat them as short furloughs for you to see the neighborhood and grab your favorite sweet treat afterward!
- **Diet**, eating too late, too much, or foods your body says "uh uh" to, concedes precious moments of rest as your body diverts that energy to digestion instead.
- **Exercise** is as powerful for your mind as it is for your body. Substitute a short drive with a bike-backpack expedition or invite a neighborhood teen for a brisk walk. Feeling sluggish or worn? Do jumping jacks for 30 seconds right where you are. It's fun, cost efficient, and you'll chuckle at your creativity to get it in!

One of the most practical and effective ways to get rest as a busy parent is to sleep when your children sleep. Let their sleep schedule be your schedule too. This advice will go against all other competing priorities in your mind. But I want to keep referring back to the premise that you are your most valuable asset. Being at your best requires sleep and rest. Everything else can wait. You will be amazed at the difference it will make immediately.

Other simple fixes:

1. Avoid physical stimulation within two hours going to bed, other than expected night routines.
2. Wake up and go to bed around the same time every day to condition your body to sleep and wake in regular cycles.
3. Create a dark, quiet environment for bedtime.
4. Do not look at the clock once you are in bed. It increases anxiety and, therefore, emotional energy, hindering our ability to snooze even more. Close your eyes and quiet yourself.

If you struggle to fall asleep within 45 minutes, change your environment. Restrict the bedroom to sleep and intimacy as a rule. Do another quiet activity like listening to an audiobook, making a cup of tea, or doing a puzzle until you get sleepy. Then return to your bedroom to rest.

Key Takeaways

- Keep doctor visits on the schedule as planned and make them enjoyable.
- Try to have at least one hot balanced meal per day. Or stock up on fruits and vegetables, healthy snacks, and a protein substitute to keep you going all day. Store them in places of easy access (fridge, car, purse, home office). Eat your last meal before 7p daily.
- Reserve your room for rest and romance only.
- For insomnia, don't look at the clock. Leave the bedroom for another quiet activity until you are sleepy. Then return to the bed.

9

Stimulants

When healthy, we become tired or even sleepy by the end of a fulfilling day and sense a feeling to rest after exerting ourselves physically or mentally. By meeting the need to rest regularly and properly, we meet the demand of our body to rest. After resting, we are reinvigorated and are ready to work more.

But sometimes we push ourselves beyond the hastening of our body to rest through the use of stimulants (like caffeine or sugar). Stimulating our brain to go beyond its internal restraints is not a substitute for rest. Using caffeine as a substitute for the nap you'd prefer to take is an easy way to feel hit by a train later when the stimulant wears off.

Generally, when adults work, we become tired, weak, or sleepy and require rest. But in this new age of technology and advances in medicine, parents, teens, and workers often force their bodies to continue activities after fatigue demands a halt.

Relying on caffeine to keep yourself awake or alert after your body has told you it needs rest can result in a wide range of problems, from inability to "turn off" your brain, headaches from deprivation of caffeine, and dehydration.

While stimulants are not bad in and of themselves, they create a temptation to use more energy than your body has in store. Imagine you are an iPhone, and when you click "ignore" to the "10% battery left" warning, your body just shuts down and you fall asleep like a narcoleptic! You can't "shock" your phone back awake or shake it for extra battery. It has to recharge. Our bodies want us to do the same. Instead of hitting "ignore" at 10% battery in your body, take the warning seriously and excuse yourself to take some time to rest.

There's a reason that children don't need stimulants: they take naps. During infancy and childhood, play and other early childhood activities are a regular engagement. Children wear themselves out, become fatigued, and are forced to rest. After their body restores itself, they pop back up, ready again to conquer the next task with enthusiasm and renewed excitement. That's why toddlers seem to have boundless energy.

An example of a good stimulant that can have a positive impact is looking forward to something. For example, you may be tired after work or a long day with a very active toddler. But at 5:00 p.m., you are enthusiastic and energized at the sight of your spouse and an impending date night.

Travel, or a complete change in scenery, acts in the same way. Grab a great book or a creative calm activity. A few hours away from the home and children. Value these moments in time.

Key takeaways

- Stimulating our brain to go beyond its internal restraints is not a substitute for rest.
- Workers often force their bodies to continue activities after fatigue demands a halt.
- An example of a good stimulant that can positively impact your day is a change in prospect—looking forward to something.

10

The TV Is Not My Friend

I don't generally watch much TV, but one day I felt the need to watch a show. I enjoy wholesome TV, cooking shows, home improvement, and public broadcast documentaries - shows that allow my mind to relax and block out the many to-do's just beyond the living room walls.

During early days of parenting, I gradually found it easier to escape into this 'happy' land where everything had a predictable ending. TV made me laugh. It didn't wail at all times of the night or spit up or require diaper changes. My viewing progressed from news and home decoration to dramas and court shows. What I found novel and entertaining at first quickly became a new part of my daily regimen, an urge that needed scratching. The TV watching hours piled up from 1 to 3 to maybe 5 a day. I made the excuse that I needed the rest. I deserved the rest. Dramas and love stories became my preference, and the hours of much-needed rest and reality were diverted to a billowing cloud of fantasy. I became noticeably more irritable at my surroundings. My home was not like the nice, neat, and expensive surroundings I saw on the TV series. My husband was not nearly as handsome or strong or educated as that lady's husband on the show. My attitude grew bitter and discontented and ungrateful.

One day I was watching what had become one of my favorite shows. My two-year-old at the time wanted attention. She put a book in my lap to read to her. I did not want to read at that moment, so I ignored her. She tapped my lap again, and again, and again, saying, "Please read Mom, read." My irritation grew until I yelled, "What?!" My voice was stern and much louder than I intended. Her tiny body jumped, and her eyes welled up with tears. She just stared at me, wondering who this woman was, and where her mom had gone. The look in her eyes cut me to the core.

I pulled her in to my chest and hugged her tightly as I started crying, too. I was so ashamed of my behavior and what I had allowed myself to become. I noticed that it was 4pm, which meant I was behind on dinner, I had missed a commitment at 2pm and worst of all, four hours had passed without cognizance. That day I set limits on what I watched and when, and made a note of suspicious signs of addiction to TV watching for future use.

Embedded in this failure of mine are many lessons about how we chose to use our down time. Entertainment is designed to lure you into a place where you don't have to think. Like everything, taken in moderation, TV and other entertainment can be enjoyable and helpful. However, when you least expect it, dangers in misuse of TV watching could carry you down an unexpected path. Monitor your engagement in entertainment to ensure you don't lose countless hours of your day, neglecting other needful tasks.

Another subliminal danger is believing that the fantasy life of fame, fortune, or beauty the media portrays can and should be yours by adhering to their formula. The more you watch and are entertained by a false narrative, the less appealing your reality becomes. You should be careful not to adopt the behaviors, speech, thought patterns, and deviant acts portrayed as funny or harmless on TV, when in truth, these are both self-sabotaging and hurtful to others. We can become jaded to the effects of foul language, violence, and sexual content as they have become the norm in our society. It is a very slippery slope. Soon, it becomes "not so bad" for us to adopt foul language, violence, promiscuity, etc. in our own homes, in front of our children, and in our marriages. The same caution is appropriate for social media.

Apple has a new feature in many of their products that allows users to track their screen time. It can be a wake-up call when you get the notification that you spent upwards of four hours on your phone on a particular day! Unfortunately (or perhaps fortunately, if you are like me and prefer not to know), TVs do not keep track of screen time. This is likely to keep you watching and avoid the action I'm going to challenge you with next: turn it off!

Keeping track of how much TV you watch is a way of keeping track of time waste. There are benefits to some TV—staying informed, having a laugh, unwinding from the day—but it should not be a staple in your day-to-day functionality. We (consciously or subconsciously) rely on televisions in non-beneficial ways. TV becomes a crutch to the weary or unaware parent at home. To see how entangled you have become, try to turn the TV off during your favorite show and see what resistance you feel inside.

The stay-at-home parent should be particularly cautious about the amount of TV watched because it means you're choosing TV over potential time or planning for your children. I'm not talking about watching one show during your evening bedtime routine, or waking up with coffee and a show. I'm speaking to those who keep the TV on all day. We become so accustomed to it, we hardly notice how it can distract us from giving our children full attention. Maybe you're feeling tired simply because your brain is subconsciously multitasking by watching the TV and your kids! Use valuable daytime to think through problems, or planning, or writing in a journal, or creating crafts for the little ones.

Simply having the TV on as background noise is a potential source of exhaustion, but more so is the content of the shows we keep on all day that perhaps make us more tired. A Psalmist in Chapter 101 said that he would "set no evil thing before his eyes" (v. 3). Seemingly harmless shows, when repeated over and over day after day, can begin to instill ungodly traits, like crude language, sexual conversations and inappropriate humor, bashing of values you'd like your family to embody, and more. While these all may be in "jest," it is not a laughing matter to God. Furthermore, even "innocent" or "clean" shows can perpetuate unrealistic standards for mothers, fathers, marriage, children, and parenting.

When we choose this "world" of hypothetical drama, humor, and "utopia" over our own reality, our families suffer.

Key takeaways

- Set limits on what to watch and when and make note of suspicious signs of addiction to TV.
- Monitor your engagement in entertainment to ensure you don't lose countless hours of your day, neglecting other needful tasks.
- Another subliminal danger is believing that the fantasy life of fame, fortune, or beauty the media portrays can and should be

yours by adhering to their formula. The more you watch and are entertained by this false life that may be quite different from your own, the less appealing your reality becomes.

- Avoid adopting behaviors, speech, thought patterns, and deviant acts portrayed as funny or harmless on TV, when in truth, these are both self-sabotaging and hurtful to others. TV becomes a crutch to the weary or unaware parent at home.
- Entertainment is designed to keep us intently engaged for endless hours.
- If signs of addiction to TV surface, turn it off.
- Limits placed on TV exposure and content will keep you on target for tasks.

11

The Enemy Encourages Exhaustion

God made us stewards for our children—to teach them godly morals, values, and behavior. However, even from the beginning, there was a snake in the garden, spinning His words to trip us up. Battles are waged against us that constantly, consistently, and systematically work to devour our health, families, children, and spouses. It is an unhealthy mindset, religious spirits, or people pleasing that convinces us that the only way we are truly putting others first is by sacrificing our own health. The more exhausted we become, the more susceptible we are to falling into these self-sabotaging traps. The habits of unhealthy eating, lack of rest, snappy remarks, and emotional absence from our children and spouses are all results of the enemy's interference in our body's urgent signals to rest.

As our Provider and Protector, God has set guardrails in place to deter many of these attacks, with weapons for defense like Scripture, prayer, fellowship, community, and even fasting.

- o Reading Scripture roots us in truth, re-centering our perspective in light of Christ.
- o Prayer is the application of Scripture, allowing ourselves to be held, loved, and cared for by our own Father.
- o Perhaps the most overlooked aspect of living a godly life is maintaining a community of believers. We are not meant to be parents without a support system. Meeting even monthly with

others who support and care about your faith will do wonders for your mental and spiritual health.

o   Even fasting—the deliberate act of acknowledging how God is our ultimate bread of life—can help plant our feet in Him.

The agenda of the enemy, coupled with our own temptation and ability to create physical and emotional stress beyond what we can handle, wreaks havoc on our mental processing throughout the day. If we are not sleeping well, and constantly consuming drinks and foods that stimulate us, severe damage can occur to an already-fragile body.

Our body is the temple of the Holy Spirit. We are responsible for its correct use. It returns the favor by being a vehicle to carry out all that our minds can think and do.

Key takeaways

- It is an unhealthy mindset, religious spirits, or people pleasing that convinces us that the only way we are truly putting others first is by sacrificing our own health.
- The more exhausted we become, the more susceptible we are to falling into these self-sabotaging traps.
- The habits of unhealthy eating, lack of rest, snappy remarks, and emotional absence from our children and spouses are all results of the enemy's interference in our body's urgent signals to rest.

12

God Promises Us Rest

In Psalm 37:7, we are told to rest in the Lord. It is in quiet moments that we are able to hear the Lord, resting in His embrace. When we calm our thoughts, our emotions and our bodies, we are able to hear more clearly from the Lord, who speaks in a still, quiet voice.

Scripture teaches us that we are able to calm ourselves down, and we should. In Psalm 116:7, the Psalmist admonishes his soul to be quiet. "Return unto thy rest, O my soul!" (KJV) In this verse, he is speaking to his mind, will, and emotions to take it easy—don't agitate with disquieting fears. By doing so, he reaps the benefit of peace outlined in 1 Kings 5:4: "But now the LORD my God hath given me rest on every side, so that there is neither adversary nor evil occurrent". (KJV)

During the early parenthood years, my faith was often challenged. The finances were depleted quicker than we could replace them, and our marriage was pushed to the brink. Unless we are constantly in tune with God's will for our life, we will always be trying to stay afloat. Sometimes we sink into survival mode—getting by with the bare minimum, feeling like we are in a hamster wheel. The stress of keeping up can make the days feel too short to get everything done, let alone make room for what's most important. We lose sight of the fact that our days are gifts handed down by God. We need to be in tune with God's will to ensure we are following His plan for the day. To hear His will, we need to listen. It helps to shut off all distractions—even the "necessities", and be still.

Resting in the Lord is both a privilege and a promise. He illustrates that those who believe obtain happiness and enter into this rest in Hebrews

4:3, "We, who have believed, do enter into rest..." Just as God finished His work on the seventh day (Genesis 2.2), He then rested from it. Indeed, He will allow those who believe to finish their work and enjoy their rest. (NIV).

In both the Old and New Testament, God shows His love, grace, and faithfulness by providing a safe haven of rest for us in the midst of storms. God gives us rest even amidst our enemies (Deuteronomy 12:10), from burdens (Exodus 5:5), from troubles and suffering (Psalm 94:13), from "disquieting fears" (Psalm 116:7), and from sorrow and fear (Isaiah 14:3). (NKJV)

One of my go-to Bible stories that demonstrates our humanly need for rest is in Mark 4. We meet Jesus and His followers on the Sea of Galilee, a body of water known for its sudden, violent storms.

"On that day, when evening had come, he said to them, 'Let us go across to the other side.' And leaving the crowd, they took him with them in the boat, just as he was. And other boats were with him" (Mark 4:35-36, ESV).

Before they got in the boat, Jesus had been preaching and ministering to multitudes of people. "And a great windstorm arose, and the waves were breaking into the boat, so that the boat was already filling. But He was in the stern, asleep on the cushion. And they woke Him and said to Him, 'Teacher, do you not care that we are perishing?'" (vv. 37-38, ESV) In those early days of parenthood, I had trouble keeping three humans alive and learning, but Jesus' feat was "multitudes" of crowds wanting to discuss heavy, intellectual concepts. I can't imagine how exhausted He must have been.

I bet a lot of you can relate to those on the boat. Can you imagine taking a nap during your baby's "witching hour"—an infant's own form of violent storm? I can almost hear my husband's words if I had done that: "Sonya, do you not care that I am drowning?!" It appears Jesus woke up not because the boat was filled with water, or because they were rocking in waves, but because His people called to Him for help.

I'm not Jesus, so I can't magically calm a screaming baby or a storm, but I can trust in the Father the way Jesus did. Jesus chose to rest, even in a setting where there were "tasks" to be done, people to care for, and a storm brewing around Him—taking care of others by taking care of

Himself and trusting in the Father. Because He was generous enough to be human for us, He too experienced fatigue, and He honored His body's signals. When He was rested, He calmed the waters. Peace was found on the other side of His rest.

We can try to empty our boats of water with our own hands, but ultimately it is God who will calm our storms. When we relinquish control over circumstances, even when that seems illogical, His perfect strength stills the ocean into a gentle river. You might try to steal a few moments of rest even during the storm by simply taking a few deep breaths. Don't be shy about asking that tiny overachiever "sweety, hold that thought; I want to hear the whole story, but I need just a minute to catch my breath, ok?" Or close your eyes and encourage yourself with a few words of affirmation like "I have the stamina and the wisdom required to sustain every blow. Raising my children is all a part of my purpose". Continue with words of gratitude starting with your toes. "Lord thank you for my toes. They help me keep my balance. I really like the way they are so symmetrical. You are such a good God. Thank you, Lord, for my feet. I can run, jump, and keep up with my little ones. They go fast, but I catch them every time! (smile) Lord, thank you for my ankles…" And so on, all the way up to your head. I heard someone say it is thankfulness near your knees when your attitude and perception of your situation begins to change positively, if you employ this gratefulness application. Relaying these words aloud also plants seeds of gratefulness for little ears to emulate later when they feel upset. Not to mention, it does wonders for your energy and self-confidence.

Key takeaways

- Rest is a promise from God. It is in these quiet moments we are able to hear the Lord resting in His embrace.
- When we calm our thoughts, our emotions and our bodies, we are able to hear more clearly from the Lord, who speaks in a still, quiet voice.
- Scripture teaches us that we are able to calm ourselves down, and we should.

- Unless we are constantly in tune with God's will for our life, we will always be trying to "catch up."
- Complete, pure rest comes from the grace of God.
- Our efforts to calm the storms in our lives is the impetus for rest, but ultimately it is God who will calm our storms.

13

Your Most Significant Relationships

As strange as this may sound, you should prioritize yourself over your children in some contexts. Prioritizing yourself and your health will reap positive rewards for your children. When the caregiver is at their best, the care of the children does not compete with the inner battles of the caregiver, like fatigue, demotivation, and frustrations. The energy of caregiver is self-sustaining and provides a stable aroma in the home. It feels safe to be silly, and loveable and rambunctious. And because you are in the mood to handle the day's chores with patience and grace, the children are the recipients of the sweet fruit of your labor.

Over-rotating on prioritizing our young over ourselves, our mates, or sometimes virtuous values can have devastating effects. There are wonderful and strange examples of this level of parenting in nature. Madagascar penguins are amazing creatures. After laying their egg, the female penguin, called hens, go for an entire winter in search of food while the males travel and nest their young under their stomachs perched on their feet. By the time the hen returns, their eggs are hatching, and they meet their young for the first time. The hens are ecstatic to have young to nurture. In fact, their maternal instinct is so intense, if a hen does not have young to care for, they try to find a chick (young penguin) that is orphaned to care for. Occasionally, several females chase after a single young orphan, and in their desperation, end up trampling the chick.

Humans do not trample their young intentionally. But parents can inadvertently damage their children with overprotection, crippling their ability to mature emotionally and mentally properly within the normal development stages to adulthood. Regulating the amount of control over our children includes qualifying the child's age, ability, disposition, and the situation appropriately. Focusing too much on the children tips the scale excessively towards them and away from the delicate tri-fold balance of their independence, your rest and the requirements of your significant other. The sooner you allow your child to try to effectively maintain for themselves, the more time you have to devote to yourself and strengthening your marriage.

A baby has full dependence on the parents for all of their needs for the first two years of their life. As the child grows, physical and emotional support evolves into a dependent relationship. Time passes and the nature of the relationship continues to evolve, with independent reasoning, environmental influences, and clever experimentation. The speed of maturity of the child depends heavily on the parents' ability to acknowledge their growth and make appropriate adjustments to assistance when needed. If the recalibration is off balance, the parent(s) become a crutch to the child, stifling opportunities for early development and self-reliance.

If you are married, your next priority should be your spouse. At some point, the children will grow up and move out of the house. You cannot afford to wait until then to start meeting the needs of your spouse or vice versa. Meet the needs of your spouse with compassion and commitment.

Spouses present a unique challenge when they need our undivided attention. I'll never forget one intersection of parenting and marriage that made me want to crawl under a rock.

My husband had been complaining that he didn't feel well. At the time I was so busy/overwhelmed caring for the children, the last thing I needed was one more person to care for. I struggled with pent-up anger and resentment, which manifested in apathy toward his "sickness."

Throughout the day, he helped when he felt "up to it," lying around when he did not. Throughout Friday, Saturday, and Sunday, he continued to lie down, and help when he felt like it, even though he complained that he was feeling worse. By Monday, I was a tired, frustrated, and angry woman who wanted nothing more to do with the situation.

I cooked, cleaned, did hair, did the drop-offs and pick-ups at school, gave baths, put the children to bed, and did the bills until the wee hours of the morning. After the children had left for school, he called me to the room, claiming he had severe pain. He went to the hospital and returned much later that afternoon.

When he returned, he told me that the doctors found a thrombosis vein, or what is commonly known as Deep Vein Thrombosis (DVT) —a potentially life-threatening condition. DVT is a blood clot that causes excruciating pain. The doctor performed minor surgery for its immediate removal.

Needless to say, I felt like a horrible spouse, and realized I would want to be treated better if I'd been in his shoes. I realized I needed to refocus on caring for myself and my husband, not only the children.

Communication

> "Let the words of my mouth, and the meditation of my heart, be acceptable in thy sight, O LORD, my strength, and my redeemer." (Psalm 19:14, KJV)

You've heard it a million times, but communication is the cornerstone of a healthy marriage. Practice sharing your feelings, even if it feels silly. The best thing you can do for each other is make time and room for each other to share how you feel. If you live busy lives, it's also important to sit down each night and update each other on what happened at work, at home, out and about, and whether or not it was a good day.

Christian author Lysa TerKeurst and her counselor, Jim Cress, have often said expectations are premeditated resentments, and boy does that apply to marriage. Every few months, or even just twice a year, it's important to sit down with your spouse and walk through expectations.

- Who cleans each area of the house?
- Where does cooking dinner responsibility fall on each weeknight, a certain number of weeknights, or other ways you can tag-team?

- When the kids are sick (and both parents work), how will you decide who stays home (maybe all day or at least until you can find a sitter)?
- What's our grocery budget for the week?
- Who is watching the kids at certain times of the day?

These are the easy discussions to figure out for most people. It's the unspoken, rarely thought-of expectations that are also important to address often.

- When I'm angry, how do I want you and I to resolve it?
  - o Talking first.
  - o Taking a break first.
  - o Making cups of tea and occupying the children first.
- When I'm sad, how can my spouse comfort me?
  - o Taking the kids out for an hour.
  - o Cuddling.
  - o Looking through photos or home videos together.
  - o Giving them space.
- What are my emotional boundaries?
  - o My weight.
  - o How I cook.
  - o Listening without interruption.
- What are my boundaries with in-laws?
  - o Our private conversations
  - o Agreement on monetary support
  - o Holding each other's interests before anyone else's
  - o Prejudgment of their decisions
- What are my boundaries with the children?
  - o Unloving discipline
  - o Public or private ridicule
  - o Neglect or disregard of health or safety
  - o Profanity

All of these important discussions do not need to happen at once but communicating these kinds of expectations can prevent a lot of arguments, disappointments, and resentments.

Healthy communication opens the door to release emotions when they build. Be intentional about scheduling honest, transparent, and bilateral communication as a part of your date nights, night routine, or whenever most convenient for both partners. If you are feeling strong negative emotions when you have your partner's ear and heart, it might help to initiate the conversation with a few deep breathes, then start with "thank you for being my lover, my friend, and my confidante. I'm glad we have a chance to be together now. I'm feeling [strong emotion], but I want to be gentle, fair, and full of grace." Proceed slowly, carefully thinking through your wording. Avoid anticipating their response. Instead, exercise active listening and really internalize their response before thinking of your next point.

It helps to use the sandwich method in your statements. Start with words of affirmation, share your points of contention (1 or 2 max at a time), and end with positive affirmation or a question. A well-seasoned component of the conversation about more help in the home, and their negative response towards you, for example, might be handled like this: "honey, you are the love of my life (words of affirmation). I respect your position in our home and rely on your wisdom and strength to lead us (words of honor and respect). Sometimes I feel confused when I've worked with the children all day and feel exhausted by the time you come from work. When you come home, you must be tired too. But I need you (sharing your vulnerability) and would appreciate greater engagement with the children and help around the house. What do you think about that?" Then stop talking. Listen. Watch their body language. And pray quietly in your mind for the Lord's intervention in the messaging.

Intentionally use positive words. Keep in mind you are on the same team. Your words from the sidelines in this game of parenthood have the same encouraging nature as those of the coach, cheerleaders and fans. Words of affirmation go a long way. Also, framing your questions with 'who', 'when', 'where' and 'how' invites humility in them and in you. Have suggestions ready to go, but wait for their leadership/participation in finding the solution with you, even if you already have an answer. Here are a few starters:

- Who do you think we can call about the plumbing?
- I noticed a few late payment notices. When is a good time for us to do the bills together over a glass of wine?
- I'd love your feedback on where you recommend we register the children for daycare?
- I apologize for giving you the silent treatment last night. I'm still working through the hurt. How can I share my hurts with you in a way that is effective and safe for both of us?

Avoid 'why'. 'Why' creates defensiveness because the perception is one of blame and guilt. Even if your sweetie is clearly guilty of an offense, your role is not prosecutor or judge; you're their defender, their encourager, their helpmate. They deserve one more chance at meeting your specific well-positioned needs when you state them clearly and succinctly.

Delivery is key. Tone of voice, facial expression, body posture, eye contact, privacy and touch are all elements used in the delivery of a winning conversation or one that is doomed for failure. Pace your words. Breathe. Mirror their stance, meaning if they are standing, you stand; if they are sitting, you sit. Imagine if you are lying in bed, and your mate wants to have a deep conversation with you, but they are standing. Mismatched posturing can be easily misconstrued as aggression.

Your words are 50% of the conversation; the delivery is equally important. If you believe you cannot avoid being caustic, rude, inflammatory, profane, or provocative in speech or delivery, it's best to wait until you are able to be more balanced. Conversely, kind words of affirmation and encouragement disarms your life partner. They see you and hear you more readily. Gentle touching reinforces the bond you two have in ways that words cannot. You will sense peace and love when both partners come to the conversation to give, not just receive. Establish in your heart *beforehand* that you *will* endure the tough and honest topics until resolution, even if their honesty causes an internal 'Ouch!' Be vulnerable enough to admit your shortcomings and often ask for clarity, like "I like where you're going with that; can you say more?" Or 'thank you for bearing your heart. I'm not clear on that last point; could you please restate it?" Yes, these are 'why' statements, but they are framed so gently your partner will be pleased to answer them without feeling accused. You will gain a higher level of self-awareness from someone who knows you better than anyone else.

Communicating effectively is one of the greatest challenges for most, if not all people. Negative words are destructive and not easily forgotten. We all have to work on expressing ourselves to others constantly. Daily practice is time well-spent on the words we use and how we deliver them. When we practice regularly, we get better at it. Improvements will not only show up in conversations, but also in our attitude towards ourselves and others. During those crucial conversations, you'll find greater ease in communicating when you are emotional. Commendable results will be amplified in people's responses to you and accelerated achievements due to your eloquent articulation. And you'll both have greater peace of mind because you have dealt with strong emotions and prioritized rest as an outcome of better communication.

Date Nights

Another common piece of advice that warrants repeating is: date your spouse! In addition to individual rest, you need rest from the worries and responsibilities of life. The best way to do this is with the care and attention of your husband or wife.

Try to think of creative date nights, short trips overnight away when you feel comfortable with a caretaker, and make sure it's a balance of what you both enjoy doing. Finances and time are often the excuses for not dating each other after the wedding day, and to some degree, they are valid. However, prioritizing each other is likely a vow you made, and it deserves honoring.

Here are some out-of-the-box ideas:

- Put on a movie for the kids and set up a fancy dinner in the backyard.
- Cuddle and spend the $4.99 on a movie you've both wanted to see after the kids go to bed.
- Wake up early and eat breakfast together.

- Look for a babysitting group on social media or sign up for a babysitting service. You can also offer to swap babysitting hours with other parents.

Intimacy

The average married couple is recommended to have sex at least twice a week. There, I said it. In the middle of exhaustion, busy schedules, feeding schedules, and nightmare calls from the kid's bedroom, it's hard to make room for intimacy, but it's such a crucial part of marriage.

Intimacy is a blessing from God as a unique, physical way to express your love. It is a strong way to solidify a healthy relationship.

If you find yourselves bored, nervous, insecure, or too tired, try mixing it up! If you have to, schedule it! Try something new. Don't shy away from vulnerable conversations about what you enjoy intimately and listening to what they enjoy. Make a note of their suggestions. From time to time, ask your spouse how you are doing, to rate you on a scale from 1 to 10 (10 being best). Try not to take offense at their response, rather affirm gently "thank you for your honesty, I appreciate that. How can I improve?" When partners come to the table to give 100%, both win.

Teamwork

Marriage is teamwork when it comes to parenting. No parenting classes, marriage classes, or advice from others can prepare you for the sacrifices, chores, and messes of parenthood, but with God as your source of energy, you can build each other up, helping each other get enough rest to really participate as a family. The sum of the parts is always greater than the whole.

Key takeaways

- Prioritize yourself and your spouse over the children.
- A couple times a year, discuss expectations with your spouse.

- Healthy communication includes positive words and proper framing, as well as your delivery.
- You must rehearse clear honest communication to get better; improvement does not come organically without intentional effort.
- Make scheduled, unalterable date nights an absolute in your marriage.
- Intimacy is a crucial part of communicating love in marriage. Get comfortable discussing likes and dislikes, and ask for feedback. Continually explore ways that keep it exciting for both of you!
- Teamwork-the sum of the parts is always greater than the whole. We should come to any relationship to give.

14

Holding the Calendar Accountable

O ften tasks that require minimal effort and time from our schedule tend to escape the calendar with the logic that "it will take a few minutes." These tasks may not be low priorities but seem to cost more time to write down than to "just remember". These minutes that turn into hours are the thieves of our time. A good example is housecleaning. Many of us don't like to clean. But every now and then, things pile up and we end up having to do something about it sooner or later. The root of the problem? Housecleaning was never a part of our schedule.

Include at least thirty minutes a day for cleaning, even if you have a housekeeper. Use this time to clean small messes or to organize a drawer or two. Take care not to let small messes turn into big jobs because of accumulation. At least if it's in the schedule, you can address it on a daily basis within the confines of organization and in the interest of keeping our sanity later.

Priorities are not the only things competing for time and space. What about everything else? If something takes up more than fifteen minutes, time should be allotted to that activity. If it takes up a lot of time, that activity should be given a regularly scheduled slot. Continue to evaluate your schedule and make adjustments as necessary. Monitor activities that are consistently put off for other things; evaluate their relevance to your life and household efficiency and deal with them specifically and appropriately. Include rest as a priority that should be scheduled.

Planning periods are also a great time to begin to start new traditions for the household and revitalize others. As you schedule time to do things that you are already doing or need to do, your time is sanctioned to its activity, allowing you to concentrate on one thing at a time, doing it better, and thinking about the chore/concept, its role, and the impact in your life and others all the way through. In this regard, you become more exacting in your tasks—more purposeful. Your duties are no longer rote and scattered; but well-thought-out plans that are executed on time, with precision. It will become more difficult for you to do things "just because you've always done it that way." You'll realize that your thoughts are clearer, your memory sharper, and your words more meaningful because you have rested. Your sleep is sweet because the cares of tomorrow have been sufficiently dealt with and laid at the Master's feet the night before.

Furthermore, others are happier with you. They are happy because you are happier. Your joy will be full. Your day runs smoother because it has been planned, monies have been allocated to their respective places, and your heart is content with the certainty that things have been controlled to the degree that you are able. And the rest is up to the Lord (excuse the pun).

As you follow your new calendar system, replace all the calendar systems you own with your new time frame.

Redefining Your Daily Schedule

With pure intentions, I think sometimes we overcomplicate children's schedules, hoping to educate and expose them to new things. As they grow older, it sure does get messy, but when they're not yet in school, you are their keeper, and you can control their day. That's part of your divine duty as a parent.

Children are wired to thrive in routine. From even three months old, sleep training is recommended because even babies work best on a schedule. The more predictability you can give your child, the less time you'll end up losing to tantrums, tears, and time-outs.

Time is the most valuable commodity for a parent. Recalibration and reevaluation are the two skills required to manage the twenty-four hours in a day. To master time is to master your life. Knowing the many how-to programs, books, and mantras out there to help us manage our time won't do us any good if we don't actually put it into practice.

Time has existential value; money, relations to others, etc., can be measured. To really measure our time, we need to account for more than just the events. Our miscalculation of our time, money, and other valuable things are greatest when we don't include the prep time in our planning.

Here are steps to help you conquer that "lost time" in your day and get more rest. Be as accurate as possible in these scenarios to really discover where you have been miscalculating your time.

STEP ONE:

Write down on a blank piece of paper your top daily 5–6 priorities and the amount of time required for you to do it. This can be called your Priorities List going forward. For example:

o   Sleep — 8 hours — daily
o   Quiet time — 1 hour — daily
o   Shower/bath — ½ hour — daily
o   Eat — 2 hours total (30 min breakfast; 30 min lunch; 1 hour dinner) — daily
o   Plan the next day — 1 hour — daily
o   Exercise — 1 hour — daily

STEP TWO:

Print out one 24-hour day schedule starting with your wake-up time. The first line of your calendar is the time you actually get out of bed—not the time your clock rings, or the time you start getting out of bed. Perhaps put the time you got up this morning. All of these times should be actual. The time you block out should include travel. Start with Monday.

Sample Schedule (parent of two children not in school yet, ages 3 and 5).

TIME OF DAY	ACTIVITY	DURATION
6:30 a.m.	Quiet Time	30 minutes
7:00 a.m.	Wake up kids / allow them to leave room	15 minutes
7:15 a.m.	Cook breakfast + eating with kids (mamas, make sure you eat!)	1 hour
8:15 a.m.	Get kids ready for the day (teeth brushed, hair brushed, clothes on, morning prayer or devotion, and making beds)	45 minutes
9:00 a.m.	Play time (announce the end 15-20 minutes early so that children learn to clean up)	1 hour 30 minutes
10:30 a.m.	Snack (mamas, eat a snack too!)	30 minutes
11:00 a.m.	Room Time or Nap Use this time to clean dishes, laundry, and/or rest yourself.	1 hour
12:00 p.m.	Lunch (cooking / kids eating)	45 minutes
12:45 p.m.	Craft / Learning Time This is an independent play time (supervision required, but not as hands-on) Mamas, eat your lunch at this time.	45 minutes
1:30 p.m.	Play Time (try to get outside)	1 hour 30 minutes
3:00 p.m.	Snack	30 minutes

3:30 p.m.	Room Time or Nap Use this time to clean dishes, laundry, and/or rest yourself. If dinner requires prep, begin that now / during screen time.	1 hour
4:30 p.m.	Screen Time	30 minutes
5:00 p.m.	Second parent gets home! Expect excitement.	30 minutes
5:30 p.m.	Cook dinner – have kids set the table (or help "set" the table)	30 minutes
6:00 p.m.	Eat as a family	1 hour
7:00 p.m.	Bath time (or if not bath night, reading time. Perhaps one parent takes bath nights and one parent takes reading time on non-bath nights?)	45 minutes
7:45 p.m.	Bedtime routine (both parents involved): o Brush teeth o Go potty o Pajamas o Set out clothes for tomorrow o Read a Bible story o Pray	45 minutes
8:30 p.m.	Lights out for kids // clean up dinner (maybe husband cleans dinner while wife does laundry)	30 minutes

9:00 p.m.	Sit down with spouse and talk about the day, cuddle, and/or pray	30 minutes
9:30 p.m.	Quiet Time with God	30 minutes
10:00 p.m.	Plan the next day	1 hour
11:00 p.m.	Lights out for parents	7.5-8 hours

STEP THREE:

Take the calendar you have been using and put it alongside of this new spreadsheet. Compare Monday's scheduled activities with the actual times you have on your new calendar. What do you notice? Do you see overlap? Where have your priorities been? Document the synergies and the stolen time activities and iterate on the schedule.

Adding Variety

Plan variety in your days and weeks. Like I stated previously, children thrive on routines, so create weekly routines (i.e., on Wednesdays, you hire a sitter for the 1:30–3:30 p.m. play and snack time so you can grocery shop) so they can expect the variation. Other recommended variations:

1. On Mondays, Daddy takes kids to the park from 5:00 p.m. to 6:00 p.m.
2. On Tuesdays, Mommy takes kids to the library to pick out books from 9:00 a.m. to 10:30 a.m. (including travel time). On Tuesday nights, Grandma comes over to watch the kids while Mommy and Daddy go to church small group.
3. On Wednesdays, a babysitter (try as much as possible to use one consistent sitter for this) comes so that Mommy can grocery shop from 1:30 p.m. to 3:30 p.m.
4. On Thursdays, stay home all day.
5. On Fridays, the kids get to stay up an extra 30 minutes (or get an extra 30 minutes of screen time).

Create a game plan with your spouse for each weekend. Remember that they need rest too, so tag-team the day and make sure you have time allotted to both spend with the kids together.

I also recommend that you normalize being vulnerable with your children and letting them know you need rest too—that "room time" or "nap time" is not a punishment, but a privilege. Children are typically empathetic, and if they know in advance that parents need rest too, they're more likely to be willing to help.

Calendaring 101

A calendar is a device to help you honor your time and the time of others by recording commitments that are necessary, confirmed, and well-examined ahead of time. It should not be more than that. It should not be less than that. Events in your calendar should be deliberate and cohesive with your heart's intentions.

A calendar is not a catch-all for all events you are interested in that have come to your attention from people, emails, reading materials, or other notices. It is not a reminder of how you wish you lived your life; if should reflect your actual day-to-day dealings between yourself and others.

There is no rulebook on how one should keep a calendar, but there are endless varieties of calendars in the marketplace. Why? Because no one else can tell you how to live. Your life is a result of choices you have made up to now. And like your life, your daily living records, or your calendar, are a result of things you've decided to accept or decline as relevant to your day-to-day living.

Many people deceive themselves into thinking they have more time than they really have because their calendar is not filled with what they actually do. If this is the case, it is better not to use the calendar at all. If what you do and what your calendar is pushing you to do are different, you will always feel torn between one event and the next; you will consistently over-commit and under-deliver on most of your obligations, and you will never have the feeling of control of your day.

The calendar should operate as more of a reminder system. After you have stabilized in your thinking and time, the calendar will be as solid as you are and should (and will) become only a perfunctory confirmation of what you are already doing and a reminder system for new events added. And you become the oil that keeps the whole house engine running smoothly.

Often at the root of a very full or over-ripe calendar are unresolved emotional, spiritual, or psychological feelings or issues. Probing questions to ask yourself may reveal:

- Fear of self-reflection/self-hatred: in an effort to avoid being alone or seeing yourself, you busy yourself with activity.
- Fear of rejection: can't say "no" to others; afraid others won't like you if you turn them down.
- Lack of self-control: I can do everything that comes my way if I shift this and move this, and do this for fifteen minutes of the hour, and then go here for only ten minutes, and then … until suddenly, it's 10:00 p.m. and you still have chores, tasks, and awake children.
- Fear of marital strife: things are not so good at home or in the marriage, so you pour yourself into another person, project, or work in general to fill that void.
- Unconfessed sin: running from God.

Here are a few helpful hints in keeping a calendar:

1. Post your calendar for the entire family to see, and make sure the other parent has included your schedule alongside theirs.
2. Examine your current calendar method for effectiveness. Ask yourself critical questions like…
   a. Does this represent what I do on a day-to-day basis?
   b. Are these events important to me? Why or why not?
   c. Do I really have time for this?
3. Do not respond to an on-the-spot invite right away. Ask the person if you can get back to them. Check your calendar to see if that is a doable event considering all costs (monetary, time, travel, prep for event, etc.), think through the benefits, and then pray before responding to that individual. Very mature calendar gurus go

through this process in most (if not all) decisions to hear God's heart on the issue before committing one way or the other.

4. Always be ready to adjust your calendar if necessary as new and/ or urgent matters surface and as the Lord leads.

5. Ask yourself: What is the ultimate goal of my comings and goings? The obvious answer may be because the household requires it. But are there other subliminal goals you are working toward? Try to create a one-line family mission statement. From that, create goals that help you accomplish that mission. And tantamount to those goals are the events that make up your day that help you and your family accomplish those goals and the mission statement.

6. Layer your daily tasks. There are some tasks you can do at the same time as another, such as folding laundry and talking about your day with your spouse. Also, when a decision presents itself, be decisive and move on!

Your new calendar may not be effective immediately. It may take several days, months, and years to establish good habits with your time, resources, and energy. But with God's grace, He will begin to show you how to rebuild your life in a manner that is honorable to Him and effective for your life, and successful in the management of your home.

After you have determined how you will stretch the time you have during the day, hopefully you realize that the day is done when it is done. Continuing beyond the point where your body exhausts itself is unwise. Rest. Stop and rest.

Preparing for rest is sometimes difficult when there seems to be ever-present things to care about. Not only are they in your mind running like a hamster on a wheel, but often we see that the dishes are not done, or the floors need sweeping. Silencing the mental chatter about what needs to be done is paramount to entering a state of rest.

God provides twenty-four hours for us in one day. He loves you and wants to refresh you with sleep and rest for the next day's tasks. He knows that there are things to be done. And He will supply the wisdom and resources for you to do so. We should avoid going beyond His designated timeframe for work and His designated timeframe for sleep and rest. Either extreme is indicative of us going too far out of balance.

Key takeaways

- Take care not to let small messes turn into big jobs.
- If something takes up more than fifteen minutes, time should be allotted to that activity.
- Continue to evaluate your schedule and make adjustments as necessary. Monitor activities that are consistently put off for other things.
- Planning periods are a great time to begin to start new traditions.
- Your day runs smoother because it has been planned and money has been allocated to their respective places.
- Children are wired to thrive in routine.
- To master time is to master your life.
- Normalize being vulnerable with your children and letting them know you need rest too.
- Events in your calendar should be deliberate and cohesive with your heart's intentions.
- If what you do and what your calendar is pushing you to do are different, you will always feel torn between one event and the next; you will consistently over-commit and under-deliver on most of your obligations, and you won't have the feeling of control of your day.
- The calendar should operate as more of a reminder system.
- Silence the mental chatter to enter a state of rest.

15

Goals and Priorities

Priorities have a biblical foundation. God's plan of creation imitates a form of priority. As you read through Genesis, notice how God had an order. He made animals and man when there was a place to put them.

Priorities provide incentive. Proverbs 29:18 says, "When there is no vision, the people perish." (KJV) Many people are overwhelmed and discouraged due to pressures inside the home and outside the home. They come to church on Sunday with a smile on their face, but they wouldn't dare invite anyone in their home because it would violate the façade they present at church.

Priorities allow us to use time wisely, and as we use our time wisely, we are able to make a greater impact for the kingdom of God. Our homes need to be places where our priorities work.

Priorities need to reflect an eternal perspective. John 14:1-6 says Jesus is preparing a place in Heaven for us, and only those things we've done on earth for His kingdom will have credibility in Heaven. (KJV) Our homes are to be an earthly picture of the heavenly pattern. As you think of the priorities in your life, is your home a heavenly picture for the people who belong there?

Priorities allow us and assist us in setting goals. The reality is that strong people have goals, and weak people only have wishes. So if you find yourself saying, "I wish my house was clean, laundry done, etc.," you should make plans counting on God's direction (Proverbs 6:9 KJV). Have you taken your goals before your heavenly Father and said, "Father, which of these two or three goals would you like me to do first?" or have you just

63

done them? Get the facts and hold on tightly to all the good sense that you can get (Proverbs 23:23 KJV).

Acts 6.10 shows the speech of those that were involved indicates good practical sense and spiritual power (KJV). As you look at your life, do you have a good combination of the two—spiritual power and good common sense? We must be doers of the Word rather than connoisseurs of the Word. I love this commandment from the Lord:

"A new commandment I give to you, that you love one another, even as I have loved you, that you also love one another. By this all men will know that you are my disciples, if you have love for one another" (John: 13:33-35, NIV).

Writing down our goals and the steps required to accomplish them allows us to visualize the tasks before us and put them in order of priority. It also gives us little, bite-size pieces to work with rather than becoming overwhelmed by the whole thing.

Key Takeaways

- Priorities provide incentive.
- Priorities allow us to use time wisely.
- Our fundamental values drive our priorities.
- Priorities need to reflect an eternal perspective.
- Strong people have goals, and weak people only have wishes.
- Writing down our goals and the steps required to accomplish them allows us to visualize the tasks before us and put them in order of priority.

16

Organization and Time Management

I have never been a great time manager. It got even worse when I became a parent. I secretly envy those that are extremely organized, but deeply admire them from afar. I had a habit of being 5, 10, 15 minutes late to everything, which was disrespectful of my host's time, and an embarrassment for me and any family member accompanying me.

I remember once I went to a school function and got there 20 minutes early, only to doze off in the car and actually walk in 7 minutes late. I thought of my tardiness as irritating, but only a small character flaw that was just a reflection of who I was. Besides, the guilt and shame from being late was generally gone by morning.

Until I heard a pastor characterize being late as the sin of stealing other people's resources (time), a source of pride and arrogance, and the result of negligence and inadequate planning. Not a wakeup call I wanted to hear or believe, but it was true, and I knew it.

Belated arrivals, submissions, or commitments minimize your effectiveness as a leader inside and outside of your home. The presumptuous nature of unscheduled delays slows progress, and thus pushes other priorities outside of their designated timeslot.

A better example of grace and love would be to honor our commitments in a timely fashion by arriving no less than 15 minutes before the scheduled time. Allow time for traffic and mishaps like accidents, spills in the car, wardrobe malfunctions. A good rule of thumb is if you are 15 minutes early, you are on time; if you arrive according to the scheduled start, you are late.

There are a number of resources on time management that provide ideas. Before purchasing or downloading another resource to add to the others, consider your habits and vices, dig deep and prayerfully address the root causes. No one else knows better than you where to ascertain the gaps in your time management. Ferret out the impetus and settle into your newfound respect of time. Enjoy not having to stress about being late all the time.

Check out a variety of resources, and evaluate them from the vantage point of what's going to help you in your home. Time management needs to be pursued on an individual basis. What kinds of things are necessary to run your home? Learn what works for you. A variety of techniques can be tried and customized for your individual needs. They are not always going to work the first time, but it helps to go back, evaluate, revise your program, and go forward. Don't get discouraged if someone else's answers don't work for you. No one else can walk in your shoes. Therefore, it is critical for us to draw strongly upon the Lord to give us the wisdom we need. There are some general concepts to help you launch your time management process.

One method of productivity that has worked well for me is the practice of dovetailing or bunching tasks. Dovetailing requires some creativity. It's the process of working on two different things simultaneously. I put two or more like activities together, like washing clothes and a cleaning task close to the laundry area. Bunching is another form of dovetailing where you plan on accomplishing two goals at the same time. As you look at your goals, are there some things that have enough of a common thread that you can accomplish them simultaneously, like a call for a doctor's appointment while cooking?

To my earlier point, being mindful and focusing on one task, as opposed to dovetailing and bunching tasks, may seem contradictory, but they are not. When we are in a space where we are rested, relatively organized, and ready to seize the day, we have the capacity as caregivers to administer love and care skillfully, and stretch our efforts to accomplish some tasks that need our attention. Here's how it works. When you are operating at a pace, space, and with grace in the joy of caring for your children, and you realize "hey, I can do more right now", assess your to-do list for quick, easy tasks that you can accomplish that move you closer to your goal. A suitable task would be one that can be done virtually (on your phone or other device in close proximity to where you already are), does not take more time than you have allotted to the original task you were doing, doesn't require help of any kind, and does not require the faculties dedicated to the original task. An example of dovetailing would be washing dishes (:30 min, use of hands) and watering the lawn (1 hr, sprinklers). Another example is learning a language via audiobook while driving. A very practical example would be you realizing you haven't spent a lot of time with your toddler because the baby was fussy that day, and you decide to read the toddler their favorite book in your arms at bedtime, just you and them. Cuddles and education work well together! There are so many ways to stretch your time and resources. Make it easy on yourself by finding ways to accomplish a few things at once. You'll love the feeling of doubling your productivity score and making great use of your time and resources.

Critical to all of these management principles is the thing we tend to do last: prayer. Prayer is the resource that gives us the stamina to move ahead (Philippians 4:13, 19 KJV). God has promised to provide all of my strength and all of my needs. Jesus is the vine and I am the branch, and without him I can do nothing (John 15:5 KJV). I have to spend enough time with my Father so that I know what His marching orders are for me.

Oftentimes, the best way to make time for God is to start the day with Him rather than waiting until the day is "finished." Prayer and meditation in the wee hours of the morning has a profound impact on the rest of the day.

At times, we are excited about starting a project but do not have a plan. Adrenaline and motivation can get us part of the way, but the momentum soon wanes when we are interrupted by other things. Before you know it, there are several projects left incomplete. Continuing in this way is not sustainable, and certainly does not work when there are multiple children and you're spread thin. There are important tasks to attend to, but there should be very few tasks that are urgent. We should also discern in our lives the important and the urgent. To distinguish the two, think of level of priority on the y-axis, the 'thing' that is happening, and relations to time on the x-axis (like immediately, later, next week, etc.).

Dwight Eisenhower developed a four-quadrant time matrix[3] that helps us understand how our time is measured. Here's how its explained:

-   Quadrant 1: Important and Urgent. Examples are looming deadlines, crises, or an emergency. This is a high stress quadrant where there is an imminent risk at stake. We should avoid operating in this quadrant for an extended period of time, especially due to issues in our control (like procrastinating on a large project or causing a car accident by speeding because we're late.) Few if any items, should be in this quadrant on a day-to-day basis if good planning is in place.
-   Quadrant 2: Important but not Urgent. Bingo! This is where we should operate. Planning helps you address matters efficiently and effectively. "This is a quadrant of opportunities, opportunity to learn, to improve yourself or your relationship with people and seeing what's in store for you." [4]
-   Quadrant 3: Not Important but Urgent. Unfortunately, most of us live in this reality. How often do we prioritize things that are urgent, without considering if they are important? The travesty is postponing the important (better) thing for the urgent thing. For example, a tradition of eating dinner as a family is interrupted by a call from your boss or a text from a friend. Taking an extended call and becoming distracted as a result is a dereliction of duty to your family.
-   Quadrant 4: Not Important and Not Urgent. Time wasters. TV binging, hours on social media, etc. These are things that don't add enough value to your life to be engaged in often or for long periods of time.

Recognizing when and why we operate outside of Quadrant 2 will help us resolve fundamental flaws in our logic and set us on course for real progress. In the book *Tyranny of the Urgent*, Charles Hummel shares that our dilemma between the urgent and the important is not a matter

---

[3] "4 Quadrants of Time Management Matrix." *Week Plan*, Week Plan, 1 Oct. 2018, weekplan.net/academy/weekly-planning/4-quadrants-of-time-management. Graphic in Appendix.

of a shortage of time, but of prioritization. Very much like how we spend our money, we need to decide what's important, ascertain where our time goes, budget hours and follow through. By doing so, we identify the urgent from the important, and realize how misclassified "urgent" things had taken the place of the most important things. Once we evaluate and implement changed behaviors, we will find a ripened peacefulness in our rest and sleep.

A highly organized person can make things happen. These are Type-A personalities that you read about. Often their challenge is they leave a hurricane in their path. They get it done, but everyone else pays for it. When you are an organized person, you can be tempted to not remain dependent on God. That is why prayer must precede planning. Hummel explains Jesus as the best example of "resisting the urgent demands of others [to] do what was really important for his mission" by praying early morning while it was still dark (Mark 1:35, KJV). He prayerfully waited for His Father's instructions before proceeding each day in His life's purpose.

In light of the goals you have set, how many of them did you place before the Lord, before you take the first steps? The Godly woman in Proverbs 31 had an appropriate grip on reality of priorities in her life. She did not allow the urgent to take the place of the important in her life.

The modern businessman recognizes this principle of taking time out for evaluation. When Greenwalt was president of Dupont, he said that one minute spent in time planning saves three or four minutes in execution. Many salesmen have revolutionized their business and multiplied their profits by setting aside Friday afternoon to plan carefully the major activities for the coming week. If an executive (that is what you are in your home) is too busy to stop and plan, he may find himself replaced by another who will take the time to plan. If the Christian is too busy to stop, take spiritual inventory and receive his assignments from God, he becomes a slave to the tyranny of the urgent. He may work day and night to achieve much that seems significant to him and to others, but he will not finish the work that God has for him to do.

A quiet time of meditation and prayer at the start of the day refocuses our relationship with God. Recommit yourself to His will as you think of the hours that follow. In these unhurried moments, list in order of priority the task to be done, taking into account commitments already made. A competent general always draws up his battle plan before he engages the enemy. He is prepared to change his plan if an emergency demands it. So try to implement the plans you have made for the day's battle against the clock before the day's battle against the clock begins. Also, be open to any emergency interruption or any unexpected mishap.

You may also find it necessary to resist the temptation to accept an engagement when the invitation comes first over the telephone. No matter how clear the calendar may look at the moment, ask for a day or two to pray for guidance before committing yourself. Surprisingly the engagement often appears less imperative after the pleading voices have become silent. If you can withstand the urgency of the initial contact, you will be in a better position to weigh the cost and discern whether the task is God's will for you.

In addition to your daily quiet time, set aside one hour a week for spiritual inventory. Write an evaluation, record anything God may be teaching you and plan objectives for the future. Also try to reserve most of one day each month for assembling inventory of a longer range. Often you will fail. Ironically, the busier you get, the more you need this time of inventory, but the less you seem able to take it. You become like the fanatic, who when unsure of his direction, doubles his speed. Frantic service for God can become an escape from God. But when you prayerfully take in inventory and plan your days, it provides fresh perspective on your work.

Some time ago, a sling of bullets killed a young man, Dr. Paul Carlson. In the providence of God, his life's work was finished. Most of us will live longer and die more quietly, but when the end comes, what would give us greater joy than being sure that we have finished the work that God has given us to do? The grace of the Lord makes this fulfillment possible. If we continue to properly plan, He will free us from the tyranny of the urgent, making room for rest and revitalization. Consistency and proper prioritization will free us to do the important, which is the will of God.

Let's look at principles that will assist in the selection of our priorities. The first is:

1. The principle of obedience – in those areas specifically addressed by the Bible, the revealed commands of God are to be obeyed. As a reminder to us as women, we need to continue to look at the priority of the home as established by God. We should never do

wrong to make a situation right. We have a responsibility to obey God's word.

2. The principle of freedom – in the areas where the Bible provides no command or principle, the believer is free and responsible to choose his course of action. But we cannot choose that course of action without spending time on our knees.

3. The principle of wisdom – in non-world decisions, the goal of the believer is to make wise decisions on the basis of spiritual expediency; what is best going to further the kingdom of God.

4. The principle of humility – in all decisions, the believer should humbly accept in advance the outworking of God's sovereign will as it touches each decision. God does not make mistakes. He is sovereign. We can have the plan all set out and it does not work. We need to learn that He is the One in control and we are not. Fairness is not a Biblical principle; humbly accept His will.[4]

Personal Planning Pointers

Start by starting. There is no better time than right now to evaluate how you spend your time and figuring out where you can prioritize your health and rest. Here are a few self-starters that you can start to integrate into your daily routine.

1. The longer the planning period that we have, the less detailed the plan needs to be. But the plan still needs to be in its skeletal form.
   a. Plan the predictable and leave ample time for the unpredictable.
2. Work smarter, not harder.
3. Do the difficult tasks when you are at your best.
4. Do small jobs regularly to avoid doing bigger, more time-consuming jobs later (e.g., clean spills right away).
5. Delegate whenever you can; the virtuous woman in Proverbs 31 delegated. Try saying "No." A gracious woman retains honor. Refusing graciously is good and right, but it's alright to say "No" as well.

---

[4] Hummel 1997, see Bibliography.

6. Think ahead, schedule regular maintenance projects and renewal priorities on your calendar.

7. Do big projects in small pieces rather than being overwhelmed or coming up short in the end.

8. Don't wait until the deadline; there are very few things that have to be done at the last minute.

9. Anticipate needs for upcoming projects. A lack of foresight results in wasted time and resources.

10. Avoid rush hours when you can allow enough time to compensate for it.

11. Avoid impulsive errand running; set a time and do several together.

12. Take time every night to prepare for the next day.

13. Don't trust your memory. Write. It. Down. Any prior plans, appointments, etc. should be written in a place that you can find it, and then check your priorities, calendar, etc. before making new commitments.

14. Conserve and control time.

15. Set deadlines; if someone else isn't imposing deadlines, set them yourself.

16. Handle paper and correspondence once.

17. Deal with distractions and interruptions swiftly without drifting from your priorities. "Not right now" works really well in these cases.

18. Develop conversation closure where you politely indicate that you need to end the conversation, graciousness but firmness. Telephone conversations can kill us. Tame the telephone; it should be a time-saver not a time-killer.

19. Avoid people who waste time.

20. Determine objectives (intermediate goals) for meetings and appointments and work towards them.

21. Keep a personal time log; find out how you use your time vs. how you think you use your time.

22. When you have to wait, keep projects handy that you can do. Travel time? Listen to a book, music, or talks that encourage you.

23. Make evenings and weekends count towards progress, but allow for flexibility if you need rest.

24. Strike a balance; estimate a reasonable routine, not a rigid rut.
25. Pace yourself. Don't push; understand what your limitations are and work within those parameters.
26. Be flexible but not undisciplined.
27. Be spontaneous but not unscheduled.
28. Proctor the three Ps:
    a. Procrastination: the thief of time that happens when you put off the inevitable.
    b. Perfectionism: Recognize that you can't be perfect, nor can your house, spouse, or children. Focus on creating the best quality you can within your parameters.
    c. Poor Punctuality: This is the thief of others' time. Try to be early.
29. Give yourself a break; learn to live with loose ends, reward yourself with completed tasks (realistic), and enjoy life.

Your priorities, goals, and time use must serve a purpose—the purpose God has called you to. If you go against the person that God has made you to be, you will deplete your energy and deplete your time because you are expending it in the wrong direction. You are fearfully and wonderfully made. Do not lose your identity of who you are and who you belong to.

Key Takeaways

- We honor our commitments in a timely fashion by arriving no less than 15 minutes before the scheduled time.
- Plan the predictable and leave ample time for the unpredictable. Consider your habits and vices, dig deep and prayerfully to address root causes of tardiness and missed appointments.
- Dovetailing is the process of working on two different things simultaneously. Bunching is another form of dovetailing where you plan on accomplishing two goals at the same time.
- Critical to success of all time management principles is prayer.
- Of the four quadrants, recognizing when and why we operate outside of Quadrant 2 will help us resolve fundamental flaws in our logic and set us on course for real progress.

- The dilemma between the urgent and the important is not a matter of a shortage of time, but prioritization.
- A quiet time of meditation and prayer at the start of the day refocuses our relationship with God.

17

Counting the Costs: Family Finances

Part of planning the calendar is the tedious task of planning finances. As we realistically grapple with the exhaustion of parenting, we need to recognize the capacity of financial fatigue.

On our wedding night, we knelt in prayer together and gave our marriage and future children (by name) to the Lord. We agreed to my not having a job and raising our children until they had the ability to speak on their own. We moved from the east coast to the Midwest to start our new life as a married couple.

My husband was the only one working. Our small, one-bedroom apartment was all we could afford, but we were content with our decision not to carry debt from our wedding. We paid monthly car payments to his parents for a salvaged Ford Taurus they bought at an auction for us. Although we didn't have much, I enjoyed managing the finances and made paying down debt and increasing our credit scores a personal project.

Three apartments and two years later, we still had not conceived, so I took a full-time job. Curiously enough, we did not save any money for children; I did not anticipate costs associated with birth, car seats, school, or any of it.

Our first child came early at 23 weeks. The hospital social worker shared that the bill for our daughter's care in the NICU was so excessive they called her the 'Million Dollar baby'.

The hospital bills were only the beginning. We used our savings and some investments to purchase a home before our daughter was released to come home. Unfortunately, I left work more than four months before my scheduled maternity leave so we did not have much money saved. The expenses for a car seat, formula, and diapers racked up quickly under our new single income. Then another miracle happened. We were expecting again, this time twins. We were skeptically optimistic that we could make it work financially. The prenatal care was primarily covered, but we now had a baby, food, baby clothes, maternity clothes, and still had no furniture for the house.

The twins were delivered at 36 weeks. They were beautiful! Now we had three children under the age of one. The weekly diaper, formula and wipes bill was about $700 a month, alone. The mortgage was $2500. And food was around $1000 a month. We couldn't afford new clothes, so we bought clothes second hand. There was no money left after the paycheck. Not for a sitter, or eating out, or home repairs and certainly not enough for entertainment.

After squeezing every penny we could from our savings and earnings, we prayerfully considered a new job offer that was significantly more money, but would take my husband out of the house during the week. Little by little, we purchased a piece of furniture here and there, a van for our tribe, and scheduled a few field trips with the kids. But our marriage took a beating. And so did my rest. I steadily sank into a world of two to three hour rests a night. I did not have the wherewithal to see my own emotional bankruptcy.

According to Scripture, children are a reward. Psalm 127:3 states, "Lo, children are a heritage of the Lord: and the fruit of the womb is his reward" (KJV). There are many things we can do to earn a reward in today's world. But what can we do to "earn" a child? The answer is nothing. God's sovereignty determines childbirth, the number of children, the finances—all of it. Additionally, this verse refers to children as His heritage, often referred to as His legacy or birthright. Clearly, children are viewed in God's eyes as invaluable, indispensable, and highly cared for individuals. Since God created children, He will provide the means for us to take care for them, I thought. So often, God's provision seemed more minimal than abundant for the lifestyle we chose to have or keep.

Soberly consider the pros and cons when making a decision about having children, the timing, and how many children are affordable based on your current income. Also be transparent about how you can prevent unplanned pregnancies and walk through a month's finances prior to having (more) children.

Perhaps God's means of getting your attention is by simplifying your life from a dual income to a single-income household. Any resistance to His will in this regard will not reap long-lasting peace and ultimate satisfaction in your life or the lives of your family. Unfortunately, it will be the children that will pay the most for a decision of this magnitude. And your sleep, peace, and rest will suffer.

The following is a questionnaire that will help guide you and your spouse in discussing where you are financially, where you want to be, and what needs to change:

The Black-and-White Questions:

1. How much do we (both) earn per month?
2. How much money is spent on recurring bills per month?
   a. Car payment or transportation?
   b. Gas/Electric?
   c. Water?
   d. Internet?
   e. Student loans?
   f. Mortgage or rent?
   g. Credit cards?
   h. Phone (line and payment plan)?
   i. Car insurance?
   j. Renters (or home) insurance?
   k. Health insurance (if independent from work)?
   l. Childcare?
3. How much money is spent on groceries and gas per month?
4. Do we need to start incorporating babysitting money into the budget?
5. How much comes out of our bank account in total per month?
6. How much credit are we using per month?
   a. What does our credit score look like right now?

7. How much money is spent on optional items per month?
8. How much are we saving per month?
   a. Kids' schooling
   b. Retirement
   c. Unpredictable expenses
9. How much are we tithing per month?
10. Will I be getting a raise, bonus, or tax return? (for working parent)
11. What are the bi- or tri-monthly costs to budget?
    a. Oil changes
    b. Kitchen, bathroom, laundry, and cleaning supplies
    c. Doctor co-pays
12. What are the yearly anticipated costs to budget?
    a. Tax season
    b. Car repairs
    c. Home repairs
       i. Furnace
       ii. A/C
       iii. Appliances
       iv. Plumbing
       v. Electrician
13. How much can we afford to spend on…
    a. Birthdays
    b. Graduation parties
    c. Weddings
    d. Back-to-school
14. What memberships do we pay for?
    a. Streaming services
    b. Music services
    c. Amazon Prime
    d. Magazines
    e. YMCA
    f. Community pool, tennis clubs, etc.

The Feelings Questions

These next questions are more introspective. Talk about your feelings, concerns, and the ways God has blessed you.

1. Am I (are we) happy with or confident in how we spend our money?
2. Is there any area we need to cut back on in order to meet needs, not wants?
3. What discouraged me most about budgeting in the last section?
4. What made me happy about our budget in the last section?
5. How have we been challenged financially in the last year?
6. How has God blessed us and taken us through each financial challenge?
7. Am I fulfilled by my job (or my stay-at-home parenthood)?
8. Do I feel overworked, underappreciated, or uninterested in my job?
9. Was the last section of budgeting news to me? (I.e., should I be more involved in budget decisions?)
10. Are there any undealt-with resentments about spending habits of my spouse?
    a. What happened?
    b. How did it make you feel?
    c. What's a compromise or resolution for next time?
    d. Am I being too controlling or too relaxed about my spouse's spending?
11. How should we approach talking about money in front of or to our children?
    a. Should we teach them about tithing? At what age?
    b. Should we teach them about savings? At what age?
    c. Should we start giving them allowance for their chores? At what age?
    d. How much are we open to spending on their wants vs. how much they need to spend with earned money?
12. What do you appreciate the most about how your spouse handles money?
13. What is one unexpected blessing from the last year?

Whether you're barely making ends meet or wondering how to best use all the blessings God has bestowed and trusted you with, contemplate each decision thoroughly. We're going to talk more about finances in the next chapter, so please be prepared to apply the answers to these questions to the next section. I know it can be exhausting, but failing to plan is planning to fail.

Write your answers and date the responses. Reflect on them at each junction of your family's evolution. Each milestone has its own unique nuances, everything will change. From infants to toddlers, preschool to elementary, middle to high school – the financial components will shift based on the priorities.

Whether you have no children or multiples like we did, financial stability is always top of mind. After being reduced to one income from two, a new mortgage, and a traveling spouse, we relied heavily on the wisdom of God to direct our paths, and worked together to meet each challenge, one at a time.

During the infant stages, we saved by taking advantage of buying items in bulk. We became members of large chain that sold in bulk. We purchased meats, milk, bread, and other daily essentials, divided them into meal sizes, labeled and froze them in a large freezer I purchased second hand. We saved money by reducing trips to the store during the week. I did not have time to be a coupon-ista, but I did check the Sunday papers for coupons, cut and filed them for items purchased regularly.

Another hefty expense category was paraphernalia for the children – car seats, high chairs, strollers, and cribs. I joined a local mom's networking club and made large purchases at swap meets and children's secondhand sales. I was sure to take good care of my purchases so they would be in very good condition for resale. Children grow so quickly out of their clothes and shoes, I would also time local store merchandise rotation at the end of a season for sale items, and buy two sizes bigger than they were at the time.

My industrial nature delighted and humored my husband who joked that we would never run out of anything. But the Lord also blessed me with a master craftsman as a partner who built shelves so I could store the extra food, and who delighted in fixing things around the house. I can't imagine how much it would have costs if he were not so handy. There may be people in your social circle that enjoy repair or building things. Connect with them and see if there are budget-friendly solutions you can negotiate.

Early childhood parenting in our home was not easy mainly because our finances weighed heavily on my mind. But as I looked at how happy and care-free our children were, I knew beyond a shadow of a doubt the Lord had us in the center of his will, and that He would provide for us. I could see God's grace in rewarding our frugality with a nice bonus here, a refund check there, and surprise gift from loved ones somewhere else. He responded to our faith by providing in strange and unexpected ways, and remained faithful to His promise to us on our wedding night.

As individuals, our time was as constrained as our budget. I took for granted my single years of spend thrifting on vacations, shopping, and hanging out but made up for it during early childhood years. I learned to do my own hair and nails, and shopping for myself was out altogether. Every now and then we would reward ourselves by ordering a pizza for family night or going out to dinner for our date night. Those occasions were even more cherished because they were so rare. We'd giggle like school children as we raced to the car for a three-hour hiatus from our busy lives. Quite frankly, I think we missed each other as individuals, and basked in cataclysmic euphoria in the local seafood restaurant.

After potty training, a different 'busy-ness' monopolized our time and money as they got older. I became more adept at selling and saving. As tight as our finances had been in the beginning, we finally started to feel our work paying off – literally. I was taking freelance jobs writing and selling products. I also brought in a little income working as a bookkeeper for a few small businesses in the area. We trained our children to start to clean up after themselves, fix their beds, and made fun songs to help provide direction for self-care. No, they were not perfect and yes, sometimes the mess doubled and I'd end up cleaning more than if I had done it myself. But at age 4/5, they were capable of starting small chores, managing some self-care like brushing their teeth, and taking care of their things. Remember, the goal is for you to rest. You do this by handing off chores as quickly as you can to the children, even in small chunks, until it is off of your plate. The lighter your load, the more freedom you have to do other things.

Eventually, we climbed out of more debt and built a small savings with still one income. The children were a little older and even more delightful. I started a small business working from home as we prepared to send our children to preschool. But before preschool, we had to learn the hard lessons of daycare.

Key Takeaways

- Soberly consider the pros and cons when making a decision about having children, the timing, and number.
- Discuss issues openly to understand where you are and where you are going.
- Failing to plan is planning to fail.
- Smart money management like buying in bulk, couponing, and taking temporary short-term jobs to supplement the family income eases the financial burden, and is the mark of a wise steward of time and money.
- Plan for regular cash flow hits beforehand like expensive baby gear, babysitter services, and large purchases like a car or a home.
- No matter how it looks realistically, the Lord is working behind the scenes to provide for you.
- Evolving milestones in a child's growth brings associated changes in family finances, priorities and trade-offs. Take advantage of the shifting seasons and refocus your efforts to regain momentum.

18

Lost, Lonely Eyes: Making Decisions About Daycare

Whether you're a stay-at-home parent, dual-income household, or single-income household, parenting is expensive. One avenue that a really exhausted mama (or daddy) might consider is procuring childcare.

The negative stigma around re-entering the workforce after having children has subsided, but it's worth repeating that neither staying at home nor working make you a better or worse parent. They're just different directions parents take as a result of knowing what their children need the most.

Our children certainly struggled with daycare, but it was a decision I had to make for my own health and well-being.

Although my husband would come home after work and start dinner, relieve me for a nap or shower, or just take on childrearing duties for a few hours, I did not have the energy, stamina, or willpower to nurture my own well-being in those early days of parenthood.

About a year after starting our family, my husband took a job that required travel during the week. Consequently, not only was my help gone, but also my closest companion. After the birth of the twins, I spent several months looking for help, but never found the right situation. The job of caring for three children under the age of two during the week alone became exasperating.

I reached my limit in maintaining my emotional and physical health, as well as a healthy attitude toward my husband and my children. I sought the most affordable and readily available outlet: daycare. I felt I had exhausted all other avenues available to me. With no family closer than three thousand miles, options were limited.

There were the "mal-committers," a term I made up that describes people who committed to helping in one form or another, but for whatever reason, had not followed through. There were so many people in our lives that fit this category, it seemed impossible to trust anyone to do anything. Repeat offenders were sentenced to probation in my mind. Future dealings with these persons were cordial, yet distanced due to my unforgiving, exasperated mind. They were given only restricted access to our lives for a time—partly because I did not have the energy to nurture that relationship, and partly because I had a difficult time forgiving and forgetting in my desperate need for help. Unfortunately, a lot of the repeat offenders were close to us and certainly knew of our desperate situation but continued to make and break promises.

I made the decision to find an affordable daycare out of sheer exhaustion one day. Unaware of what was happening, the children got dressed, singing merrily and laughing with snacks. I felt scared and guilty when I drove into the daycare parking lot but saw no other way to get the help I needed to rest. When it was time for me to leave the children in the hands of the daycare worker, I turned towards the door and took a few steps. Each child dashed towards me, screaming at the top of their lungs in agony, grasping my legs as if their life depended on it. Their faces reflected this intense horror, with tears streaming down their red faces. The teacher peeled them off of my legs one at a time and restrained them as I closed the door behind me. I could hear the echo of their terror even in the parking lot. Guilt overwhelmed me as I sat in the car, trying to convince myself that this was the only way for me to gain any sense of well-being. I sat there - stunned at what I had just done. I became nauseated and opened the door in agonizing regurgitation. Then I wept. I felt like a failure. Was I sacrificing my children for my own relief? I felt trapped, knowing that taking them out of daycare was not a good solution; but my heart ached with the alternative of leaving them behind.

Later that week, the daycare allowed parents to visit anytime during the day to observe unseen how their child was integrating into the classroom. I took advantage of this opportunity because I really wanted to know how they were adjusting. I was told that this was the first time the caregiver was finally able to put them down without them crying. Sullenly I observed my two-year-old. She wandered around the play room without the smile and bounciness I was so accustomed to seeing. Her eyes were blank and dark as she seemed to float from one place to the other, looking, wandering. Her lost, lonely eyes seemed void of purpose and direction, seeming to bide her time until the day ended.

Most of the children in that room had that same blank stare towards the things around them. I felt I had abandoned my children every minute they remained in someone else's care. This was certainly not self-imposed guilt, for the rest and revival of my soul and spirit was an absolute necessity. But it was the look on their faces when I dropped them off, when I observed them during the day, and when I picked them up that grieved me the most.

I drove home slowly. Contemplating deeply what I saw, what I felt and what they felt. The realization that we would not be returning settled in my soul as if it had been there the whole time. There was no doubt. There was no regret. There was no hesitation.

Daycare turned out not to be the best option for us. But it is an option and can be a great option for some.

Is Daycare Right for Us?

Daycare is not for every child. Some don't adjust easily even to preschool, kindergarten, and/or first grade. There are benefits and disadvantages to staying at home and sending your children to daycare before they enter public (or private) preschool.

But first let's explore options for the care of your child outside of the parent.

As a new parent, I was not aware of options outside of nannies, babysitter, or daycare. My overarching goal was to find a "mini-me" version—a person, place or thing that would duplicate *my* nurture and care systems in exactness. Friends, trust me—that doesn't exist. I searched far and wide for someone who would provide the level of care the way I did without success. This was an exhausting, expensive, time-consuming and frustrating process to endure. No one can or will do everything exactly like you. "Perfect" systems are limited based on any one person's knowledge and experiences. What we *can* control is research and due diligence in finding the best care alternatives for your family. Informed options will have cost, safety, age of child(ren) and timeframe considerations. The winning choice for you will ultimately depend on your family's comfort level in each of these areas.

A common option for childcare inside or outside of the home is babysitting. I define babysitting as a person hired to take care of all aspects of your child's welfare in your absence within a short time frame, somewhere from one to four hours. These persons generally work hourly, have lite to medium experience as a caregiver, and can be considered as short- or long-term extensions of your family unit. Prominent online caregiver resources allow for bilateral searches for families and sitters for a nominal fee. I also recommend personally vetting candidates with in-person interviews in the home, background checks, speaking with past employers, and reviewing customer ratings where possible. Frequency of interaction, personal references, and level of care you require will help you determine if they are the right choice for you.

Nannies generally have more substantial experience caring for children, combined with education or teacher training. They expect to have more long-term family interaction, and naturally enjoy the art of raising children holistically. Great nannies are coveted and can be difficult to find. Nanny agencies can help with the referral and placement process, but charge fees to do so, such as placement fees, living allowance for the nanny, and sometimes require education advancement allowances for the caregiver. A live-in nanny could be helpful for the traveling parent or one that works outside of typical first shift hours.

A daycare, or schooling in private or public institutions, is designed to handle mostly all aspects of your child's welfare on their premises from any time between three and twelve hours. Costs and services range widely but a good rule of thumb is exceptional quality plus enrollment limits equal higher costs. This rule can be applied throughout their schooling years. Services offered can range from meals, education administration, transportation, means of instruction (i.e., Montessori, environmental, etc.), staff specialties, and the like. In person interviews with potential teachers and administrators of the school will help you form an opinion that compares to current/former parent referrals. If printed information does not indicate services offered for children with specific needs, the interview would be the time to bring up concerns if you have them.

Creative options for the money conscious parent include babysitting cooperatives (co-ops). This is a network of trusted individuals who have children that swap coverage for childcare, mostly at no-cost. Co-ops can be found in neighborhood associations, parent-initiated school groups, within religious organizations, or a part of a community organization. These are very organic to the nature of the groups and can be started pretty easily. If you cannot find one and want to start one, use the contacts you have and trust and start small, with one or two families, and grow from there if necessary. Keeping it simple, fun, and low maintenance for everyone is key to sustainability.

Another opportunity would be joining a homeschool network in your area. Homeschooling can be for any age, and affords children learning catered to their particular learning style, in the comfort of the home, with peers within a two-to-three-year age range. Parents collaborate to rotate days/hours, topics, locations, and objectives based on learning topics, and other preferences. This is a great option for connecting with like-minded parents for providing specialized education of your choice for your child, a balance between hands-on care for them, and more hours of self-care for you.

Family members can also be resourceful and options for your child's care. Perhaps there are a few of you thinking "well...I don't know about that", but it's true. Having the discussion about having children and location proximity to family could surface childcare options. Whether family lives near or far, they can be resources for low or no cost childcare. Grandparents, godparents, 'adopted' grandparents, and mentors who have a history of supporting you already usually find joy and fulfillment in helping you and getting more acquainted with your little ones. For family teen cousins and college students, having food in the house and television will get you 95% of the way.

Suitable help for childcare comes in indirect forms as well. Hiring a virtual assistant (VA) is an option that could quickly pay for itself in returns on your time and effort. A virtual assistant can conduct an organized childcare search, interview viable candidates, and negotiate arrangements on your behalf. Depending on your needs, the VA can also procure home services, make appointments, plan birthday parties, and all the magnificent things you do to make your home function well. Another indirect resource of help for you is a mommy helper. Mommy helpers execute tasks on behalf of the parent that include things like grocery shopping, running errands, and depending on the arrangement, can also take care of the children at times. The advantage of having a helper like this is the chores are not expected to be centered around the children but can include them. They are an extra set of hands that can drive, lift, cook, and shop at your request.

Also explore hybrid solutions! Maybe a babysitter for Friday date nights and homeschooling Monday, Wednesday and Friday. Or combine part-time daycare daily with two-hour homeschooling on Wednesdays for foreign language study with four other parents. Any of these options give you the power of choice for when, where, and how your child is cared for by others. You don't have to duplicate you - utilize those around you to help you create solutions that allow you to rest. Or not. If you feel *any* hesitation or risk associated with any choice, seek other options that have your confidence and comfort level. Otherwise, find a way to get help with the children and around the house that allows you some downtime to recover and restore your mind and your body.

Consider the following variables in making the decision of outsourced childcare.

Benefits of Daycare

- Able to use time for rest (meditate, self-care, planning, thinking, nap, lunch with friends, bath with a book, etc.).
- Able to use time for housekeeping tasks (laundry, dishes, grocery shopping, changing sheets, taking out the trash, dusting, disinfecting, vacuuming, etc.).
- Able to reenter the workforce (pursue a new career, re-enter your old career field, study something new, or a mix of these).
- No need to plan daily activities.
- Children build social skills.

- Prepares children for preschool.
- Allows children to learn how to engage with others (teamwork and community dynamics).
- Improves marriage by lessening exhaustion, which leads to...
    o Time for intimacy.
    o Feeling fulfilled in life's calling.
    o More energy for each other.
- More energy for engagement with children when not in daycare.
- Better attitude and posture when engaging with children outside of daycare.
- Establishes routine for the children.

Drawbacks of Daycare

- Strict eligibility or limited open spots.
- Your child may be sick more often.
- Your child may not adjust well to daycare.
- Your child's sleep schedule is governed by the daycare, which can differ from home routine.
- Preferred nutrition for child may be sacrificed (if daycare does not permit packed meals, or if daycare cannot adequately assist child in eating complicated foods).
- Noticeable financial impact.
- You miss out on funny moments, relationship-building time, and developmental milestones.
- You may not have access to daycare to observe how your child is being treated all the time (there's an element of trust in daycare).
- Requires transportation to and from daycare.
- If your child is sick, at least one parent's workday will be interrupted.

Benefits of a Nanny

- Able to use time for rest (time with God, naps, lunch with husband, reentering the workforce, etc.).

- Able to use time for housekeeping tasks (laundry, dishes, grocery shopping, changing sheets, taking out the trash, dusting, disinfecting, vacuuming, etc.).
- Able to reenter the workforce (pursue a new career, re-enter your old career field, study something new, or a mix of these).
- More control over playtime, naptime, meals, curriculum, and schedule flexibility
- Able to observe care more easily.
- Able to schedule more easily.
- Less susceptibility to illness.
- More engaged and one-on-one learning.

Drawbacks of a Nanny

- Can be most expensive option depending on the level of care (live-in/live-out, level of care, your child's special needs, and care expectations).
- Difficult to find depending on where you live.
- You're welcoming them into your home, so you must trust them with your home in addition to your children.
- Fewer resources (playground, learning tools, etc.).
- If your nanny calls in sick, one of you has to stay home with the children.
- Some planning required-if your nanny plans a trip for the child, there may be safety concerns, some out-of-pocket expenses, and likely need transportation.
- Preferred disciplinary actions need to be discussed.

Let's dive into the questions you need to consider when deciding whether to do stay-at-parenting, nannying, or daycare.

- Do I understand and accept that I will miss special moments with my children for the sake of rest, productivity, and work?
- Is it financially feasible? Is there a way to compromise (i.e., part-time nanny)?
  o How much does daycare cost?

o   How much does a nanny cost?

o   How much do we earn when both parents work vs. when one parent works?

o   Do I have access to free or discounted childcare (i.e., relatives, nanny shares, babysitting swap agreements, etc.)?

- How do the children feel about the adjustment we're thinking of making?
- Is this something I'm going to change my mind about halfway through? (Because it will affect your children's stability if they're moved around too much.)
- Am I planning to have more kids?

See the Appendix for a financial worksheet to add up the costs of daycare and/or a nanny.

No matter what your family decides, know that God knows you love your children, that your children are resilient, and that you are making your decision with the best information you have at that moment. What does not work for another family, may be a lifesaver for you.

As your children grow older, you'll also gain more time to continue hobbies and pursuits inside and outside the home, especially if you are creative. This is the perfect opportunity for you to complete some of those projects you've always wanted to do but have not had the time.

God matures us as much as He matures others in their roles. If you are receptive to His gentle nudges and change from old patterns, even if it is from the least of resources (mothers-in-law, children, someone less experienced, books, and your own children), you might notice steady improvements in the home and children.

Consequently, children are used by God often to mirror our relationship towards Him. God cares about the smallest detail. He is a God of order. Since God feeds the birds and not one sparrow falls out of the sky without God knowing—how much more will our heavenly Father give His children?

Key Takeaways

- There are several outsourced options to consider. Explore what works best for your family.
- Do a pros/cons list to chart the realities of your time and resources for out of home care.
- As your children grow older, you'll also gain more time to continue hobbies and pursuits that help bring income for the family and provide an outlet of expression for you.
- God matures us in our role as parents the same way He matures others.
- Estimate the costs: time, opportunity, rate of adjustment for the child, and financial implications.
- Qualify risks to determine risk factors, your risk tolerance, and any risk mitigation measures.

19

Assembling [Your Name]

"Live life as if everything is rigged in your favor." –Arianna Huffington

At the beginning of this book, I shared a vulnerable part of my journey as a parent of multiples. Looking back, I'm grateful I did not give in to the emotional trauma of restlessness and hopelessness. I would never have gained the level of wisdom and resilience I have today. And now you are able to glean from my misgivings and create a better path for yourself. A path that is prosperous as you use the gifts you were entrusted to raise your children or grandchildren, and provide for them in ways you may not have realized. When you have prioritized your wellbeing, you will be able to give your children more than you would otherwise. You will have a bounce in your step and compassion in your heart that can handle piles of laundry, stinky diapers, and even a friend's call for prayer in the middle of the night. That is the effect of the perfect peace that God provides when you get take appropriate time to sleep and prioritize resting. You will be the instrument of grace to minister as a parent to sweet little ones who deserve your best.

We have also learned that a valuable part of your everyday life should be an element of attaining rest for your body and your soul. Embedded in that rest is a peacefulness that allows you to hear from others who may not be able to say all that's on their heart. You will be able to conduct more meaningful self-introspection to build a better 'You'. Assembling 'You' means your heart, mind, and body work in unison to maintain balance, optimal performance, and inner harmony. And you will hear more clearly from the Holy Spirit, who is able and willing to provide very specific instructions related to day-to-day tasks in the home, in your finances, and for your soul. It's that kind of wisdom that you cannot read in books or see in others. There are profound blessings in truly reflecting on what you have done and your next steps with clear thinking.

Fully digest that there is no substitution for rest, and any manipulation of our body's signals for us to slow down will result in more harm to our body. Effective implementation of healthy eating habits and cognizance of what we drink will save us from the false highs and inevitable lows stimulants vandalize from our energy. We are to avail ourselves of the potent significance of sleep. Parents and nonparents alike require around eight hours of sleep's restorative powers to prepare us for awake hours of work.

Even after learning so much about taking care of myself and my family, I am still not a perfect parent. But reprioritizing proper rest as a mandatory part of my daily routine is an extraordinary part of my healing and restoration. We strive daily to do our best and be successful in the eyes of those around us. But I find that the more I sit quietly, actively and intentionally listen, and watch others' reactions to what I do to them or for them, my knowledge deepens, and the pace at which I acquire wisdom accelerates. And after reading this book, you have tools to help you calibrate your time and duties, and minimize the crises that can happen as a result of not doing so. Practice these skills. Refer back to the exercises and chapters that pertain to your situation and use them as a guide to help you navigate your situation. Test to fail, meaning utilize opportunities to step outside your comfort zone to try something new. If it doesn't work out, you've at least learned something. You can't afford to give up; you're already in the game. Pick yourself up, straighten your crown, and try again. The world needs everything you have to offer, starting right where you are.

APPENDIX

I. FINANCIAL WORKSHEETS

	At Home	Daycare (__ kids)	Part-Time Nanny	Full-Time Nanny	Nanny Share (__ nanny rate for __ kids split between __ households)
Transportation (gas) per day					
Transportation (time) per day					
Transportation (distance) per day					
Total Transportation Per Week / Per Month					
Daily/Weekly/Monthly Fees Required (for all children)					
Groceries (food that can be packed in a lunch bag, or that someone else can easily prepare)					
Monthly Money Needed					
Monthly Money Currently Earning After Other Bills (single income) After Taxes					
Monthly Money Currently Earning After Other Bills (dual income)					
Minimum Salary					
Risk of Overbudget (one income)					
Risk of Overbudget (dual income)					

EXAMPLE:

Two children (3 and 5)
$40,000/year
$67,000/year if both working
Honda Odyssey 2007 (~30 miles to the gallon; 110,000 miles on it)
Charlotte, NC

Monthly Bills:

- $1,200 mortgage
- $200 car insurance
- $100 home insurance
- $70 internet
- $100 gas/electric
- $40 water
- $100 streaming services
- $20 trash service
- $300 to savings

—

$2,130 / month in concrete bills

Daycare Rate: $8.75 / hour
    15 miles away
    30 miles/day = 1 gallon of gas per day, $2.10 per gallon, $10.50 per week

Nanny Rate: $12 / hour
    Full Time: 8 hours
    Part Time: 4 hours

Nanny Share: $8.33 / hour
    5 kids (2 kids, 2 kids, 1 kid), 3 households, $25 / hour ($8.33 / family / hour)
    7.5 miles away
    15 miles/day = 0.5 gallon of gas per day, $2.10 per gallon, $5.25 per week

	At Home	Daycare (2 kids)	Part-Time Nanny	Full-Time Nanny	Nanny Share
Transportation (gas)	$0	$2.10 per day	$0	Depends	$1 a day
Transportation (time)	0	22 min. per day	15 min. (checking in daily)	20 min. (checking in daily)	13 min.
Transportation (distance)	0	30 miles per day	0	0	15 miles
Total Transportation: (i.e., 20 miles each way; 0.75 gallons of gas each way; 30 minutes each way = $3.00 per day; 1 hour in the car; 40 miles per day)	0	110 minutes $10.50 150 miles	75 minutes	100 minutes $15 per week on gas for nanny to do excursions	65 minutes $10.25 75 miles
Daily/Weekly/Monthly Fees Required (for all children)	0	$70/day $350/week $1,400 /month	$48/day $240/week $960/month	$96/day $480/week $1,920 / month	$66.64/day $333.20 / week $1,332.80 /month
Groceries (food that can be packed in a lunch bag, or that someone else can easily prepare)	$200 / week (for entire family)	$0/week (daycare provides)	$150 /week $600 /month	$150 /week $600 /month	$150 /week $600 / month
Monthly Money Needed	$800	$1,410.50	$1,560.00	$2,535.00	$1,942.25
Monthly Money Currently Earning After Other Bills (single income) After Taxes	$2,500 - $2,130 = $370	$370	$370	$370	$370
Monthly Money Currently Earning After Other Bills (dual income)	$4,187 - $2,130 = $2,057	$2,057	$2,057	$2,057	$2,057
Minimum Salary	40,000	40,000	40,000	Can't afford ($70K+)	40,000
Risk of Overbudget (one income)	Can't Afford	Can't Afford	Can't Afford	Can't Afford	Can't Afford
Risk of Overbudget (dual income)	Low	Low	Medium	Can't Afford	High

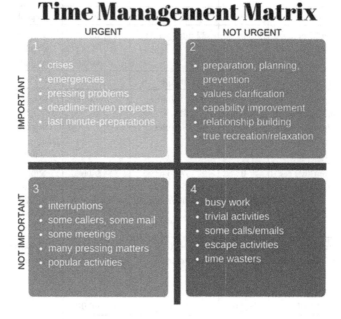

Time Management Matrix

	URGENT	NOT URGENT
IMPORTANT	**1** • crises • emergencies • pressing problems • deadline-driven projects • last minute-preparations	**2** • preparation, planning, prevention • values clarification • capability improvement • relationship building • true recreation/relaxation
NOT IMPORTANT	**3** • interruptions • some callers, some mail • some meetings • many pressing matters • popular activities	**4** • busy work • trivial activities • some calls/emails • escape activities • time wasters

- Quadrant 1: Important and Urgent. Examples are looming deadlines, crises, or an emergency. This is a high stress quadrant where there is an imminent risk at stake. We should avoid operating in this quadrant for an extended period of time, especially due to issues in our control (like procrastinating on a large project or causing a car accident by speeding because we're late. Few if any items, should be in this quadrant on a day-to-day basis if good planning is in place.

- Quadrant 2: Important but not Urgent. Bingo! This is where we should operate. Planning helps you address matters efficiently and effectively. "This is a quadrant of opportunities, opportunity to learn, to improve yourself or your relationship with people and seeing what's in store for you."[4]

- Quadrant 3: Not Important but Urgent. Unfortunately, most of us live in this reality. How often do we prioritize things that are urgent, without considering if they are important? The travesty is postponing the important (better) thing for the urgent thing.

A tradition of eating dinner as a family is interrupted by a call from your boss or a text from friend. Taking an extended call and becoming distracted as a result is a dereliction of duty to your family.

- Quadrant 4: Not Important and Not Urgent. Time wasters. TV binging, hours on social media, etc. These are things that don't add enough value to your life to be engaged in often or for long periods of time.

III.   BIBLIOGRAPHY

Hummel, Charles E. 1997. Freedom from Tyranny of The Urgent. Downers Grove, Ill.: InterVarsity Press.

The Sleep Foundation. 2020. "Lack Of Sleep Is Affecting Americans, Finds The National Sleep Foundation | Sleep Foundation". Sleep Foundation. https://www.sleepfoundation.org/press-release/lack-sleep-affecting-americans-finds-national-sleep-foundation.

"What's The Difference Between Sleep And Rest?". 2020. Thekatynews. Com. https://thekatynews.com/2020/08/18/whats-the-difference-between-sleep-and-rest/.

Printed in the United States
by Baker & Taylor Publisher Services